ANALYTICITY

# ANALYTICITY
## Selected Readings

*Edited with an Introduction by*
JAMES F. HARRIS, JR.,
*and*
RICHARD H. SEVERENS

**Quadrangle Books**

*Chicago*

Library of Congress Catalog Card Number 75-101070

# Preface

Empiricism, in one form or another, has enjoyed a long and noble history. When there appear substantial doubts about some of its most hallowed shibboleths, the occasion arises to collect some of those doubts together with the defenses they provoke. What might be called classical empiricism, best exemplified by Hume, seems to depend upon some distinction between analytic and synthetic statements. Whatever may be in fashion for casting the distinction, the core of empiricism—the notion that what we know about the world comes to us only through sensory observation—remains constant. When the distinction is challenged, the gauntlet is thrown and the time for careful reconsideration arises. Such is the purpose of this modest volume. It is intended not only for the student of contemporary philosophy, but also for the would-be classical empiricist. We hope the reader will find empiricism defunct, empiricism transformed, or classical (traditional) empiricism vindicated. Which alternative is most defensible, is for each reader to decide for himself. In any case, traditional or classical empiricism is at stake here.

There may be other reasons for doubting traditional empiricism; if neither of the following is true—that there are necessary truths which are not true of facts in the world, or that there are unnecessary truths which do have a grip on the world, and no other truths at all—then traditional or classical empiricism is in serious jeopardy. It is the purpose of the present volume to place before the reader the issues in question, and to show by example that they are not mere matters of petty word-jugglery.

Prefixed to each article is a brief summary; it is hoped that they will guide, rather than mislead, the reader.

It should be obvious to the reader that this volume would be nothing without the several contributions it contains, for which acknowledgment is most gratefully made. Our gratitude is also due to Mrs. Tensey Whitmire for her able secretarial help.

JAMES F. HARRIS, JR.
RICHARD SEVERENS

*Athens, Georgia*

# Contents

# ANALYTICITY

# INTRODUCTION

In recent years, the analytic-synthetic distinction has been severely criticized in the writings of such philosophers as W. V. Quine, Morton White, and Nelson Goodman. These men demand a clarification of the analytic-synthetic distinction, an explication of meaning or synonymy, and reject the attempts to define analyticity in terms of definition, contradiction, logical truth, or semantical rule as circular and sterile. The great amount of recent literature regarding the analytic-synthetic distinction is indicative of how seriously contemporary philosophers consider the objections of these men, and the zealous attempts from nearly every quarter to defend the analytic-synthetic distinction reflect the reluctance with which contemporary philosophers are willing to abandon this distinction. There appear to be three major considerations which might explain this concern. First, the distinction enjoys a rich philosophic tradition; the writings of Leibniz, Hume, Kant, Ayer, and Wittgenstein, among others, rely

heavily upon the analytic-synthetic distinction. Secondly, philosophers, especially empiricists, conducting contemporary epistemological inquiries employ the analytic-synthetic distinction
as an indispensable tool. Finally, the process of philosophical
analysis seems to be in jeopardy unless one assumes that the
analytic-synthetic distinction is valid.

Several major figures in the history of philosophy have made
the distinction between analytic and synthetic statements. And
though this distinction is drawn differently by different philosophers, it nonetheless still occupies a position of major importance in the philosophers' epistemologies. An examination of the
way some major philosophers have drawn this distinction will
aid in an effort to understand and evaluate more contemporary
attempts to define analyticity. Also, an estimation of the relative
importance with which Hume, Kant, and Wittgenstein hold the
analytic-synthetic distinction will emphasize the crucial role the
distinction performs in contemporary epistemology.

## LEIBNIZ

Bertrand Russell has tried to demonstrate that the entire metaphysical scheme of Leibniz depends upon his logic and analysis
of language. Consequently, according to Russell, Leibniz's metaphysics stands or falls with his logic. Whether or not Russell's
claim is true is debatable; that Leibniz's logic does occupy a
central position in his philosophy is obvious. Consequently,
Leibniz's treatment of analyticity likewise occupies a central
position.

While writing in answer to Locke in *New Essays,* Leibniz
makes the distinction between truths of reason (*vérités de
raison*) and truths of fact (*vérités de fait*). Leibniz describes
truths of reason as necessary and truths of fact as contingent. He
also singles out "primary" truths of reason which he calls identical because "they do nothing but repeat the same thing without
teaching us anything." Leibniz also tells us that truths of reason
are those which are "true of all possible worlds"; evidently,
truths of fact are those which are not true of all possible worlds.
The result is that truths of reason do not depend upon any

particular empirical fact while truths of fact depend upon some particular world being just the way that it is, that is, matters of fact. Perhaps it would not be unfair to Leibniz to introduce the terminology "analytic" and "synthetic" to designate this distinction. Let us refer to (or at least understand) truths of reason as being analytic truths and truths of fact as being synthetic truths.

Regarding primary analytic truths, Leibniz tells us that they are "*identical*, because it appears that they do nothing but repeat the same thing, without teaching us anything." [1] Leibniz intends for identical propositions to be understood in the form of "A is A" or, if not of this form, "depending solely" upon this form. Presumably, for Leibniz, the demonstration of analytic truths depends solely upon the principle of identity or the principle of noncontradiction. For Leibniz, the denial of any analytic truth will result in a contradiction—this follows naturally from the above claims.

Leibniz begins with the presupposition that all propositions are of the subject-predicate form or are reducible to that form. The predicates are (in some way) "contained in" the subject— except in the case where existence is the predicate. These predicates which are "contained in" the subject constitute a definition of that subject; consequently, the subject would be different if it had different predicates. Every true, non-existential judgment then is analytic because the predicates are, one and all, contained in the subject, but no proposition which ascribes existence to a subject (except "God exists") is analytic because existence is never contained in the concept of any subject (except God). In other words, it is not contradictory to deny that certain existing subjects exist, but regardless of their existence, it is contradictory to deny them the certain predicates which truly belong to them.

Today, the difference is marked by the appropriate uses of the existential and universal quantifiers. Whereas one can deny without contradiction an existentially quantified conjunction of a subject and one of its defining predicates, for example, ( ∃ x)

---

1. It is possible to see here the foundation for the position of logical positivism.

(x is a centaur · x is four-legged), one cannot deny without contradiction a universally quantified hypothetical with the subject as antecedent and one of its defining predicates as consequent, for example, (x)(x is a centaur ⊃ x is four-legged). This latter type of proposition is the form of analytic truths which are universal and conditional and say "*if* such and such a thing is the case, then such and such another thing is the case." To borrow one of Leibniz's examples, when one says, "Every figure which has three sides will also have three angles," one is saying nothing else than, "If there is a figure with three sides, this same figure will have three angles." [2]

When it is possible for some predicates to be contained in a particular subject (S), while this subject itself cannot be contained in another particular subject (S₁) as its (S₁'s) predicate, then this particular subject (S) is an individual substance. Individual substances have predicates which serve as the basis for spatio-temporal properties, or, in other words, the *states* of the individual substances. A subject's present and past states can and do, according to Leibniz, belong to the same subject, and the concept of the state of an individual subject is somehow contained in the concept of that individual subject.

Consider the often used but very illustrative example "Caesar crossed the Rubicon." Leibniz claims that any such singular proposition should be understood as being analytic because we would see that the predicates are contained in the subjects *if we had perfect concepts of these subjects* (of course God and only God has such concepts). Because God has such perfect concepts of all subjects, all predicates are inhered in their particular subjects; consequently, all subject-predicate propositions (which exhausts the class of propositions according to Leibniz) should be considered analytic. This points out the necessity in the connection between Caesar and his predicates, but this necessity is lacking in the connection between the predicates themselves (e.g., "Any one crossing the Rubicon is someone who conquered all of Gaul").

Leibniz's position regarding singular propositions seems to be the result of a claim that every individual substance is identical

2. See *New Essays on Human Understanding*, bk. IV, ch. II, sec. 13.

with the sum of its predicates. Now, if by a definition of "Caesar," Leibniz meant a complete listing of all the properties of Caesar, then his claim is vacuous. Moreover, this definition of "Caesar" will be nothing more than a listing of Caesar's predicates because there are no necessary connections between the contingent predicates, and, hence, if one knew all the states of Caesar up to and including time t, he still could not deduce the state of Caesar at time $t_1$—not even God with his perfect concepts. For Leibniz, "God has a perfect concept of Caesar" is the same as "God knows all the states of Caesar—past, present, and future." The important question is, does "God knows that Caesar will be in state s at time t" logically entail "it is logically necessary that Caesar be in state s at time t"? Leibniz has tacitly shifted the meaning of analytic truth from "being true in all possible worlds" or "that which cannot be denied without a self-contradiction arising" to "predetermined by God" or "that which is included in the foreknowledge of God."

Although Leibniz did not use the terms "analytic" and "synthetic," it is still obvious that he anticipated the problem of analyticity with which so much of twentieth-century philosophy is concerned, and there is perhaps no other figure in the history of philosophy whose metaphysics and epistemology are more integrally related to the problem of analyticity. In Leibniz's treatment of truths of reason one finds the seed of the claim that all *a priori* statements are analytic which was to appear much later as one of the tenets of logical positivism. Leibniz's probings into the nature of and the relationship between analyticity and ontology are indicative of the rich philosophical heritage which the problem of analyticity has in pre-Kantian philosophical writings.

### HUME

David Hume is probably the person to whom logical positivism is most indebted because the principal claim of radical empiricism has nothing to do with the question involving the origin of concepts with which Locke was concerned; the crucial tenet is Hume's claim that no verification is possible without an appeal to sense experience. An examination of Hume's theory regarding necessity and contingency will reveal just how appropriate it is to attribute this position to him.

As is well known, Hume divides all objects of human reason or inquiry into *relations of ideas* and *matters of fact.* Included as relations of ideas are the disciplines of geometry, algebra, mathematics, and logic. Affirmations are made in these disciplines of which one is "intuitively or demonstrably certain." Relations of ideas are known by "mere operation of thought" while matters of fact are founded on the relation of cause and effect.[3] Although the denial of a relation of ideas is self-contradictory, one can deny a matter of fact with no contradiction.

For Hume, the propositions of mathematics are not well-confirmed empirical generalizations as they were for John Stuart Mill; consequently, Hume was certainly not an empiricist in the sense in which Mill was, so far as mathematics is concerned. All the propositions of mathematics involve relations of ideas according to Hume; their truth or falsehood depends entirely on some necessary connections among ideas. At least in this sense, Hume agrees with the rationalists; the propositions of mathematics are necessary and are not heavily confirmed inductive conclusions as Mill claimed. Indeed, Hume maintains that mathematics is the only science in which one can retain exactness and certainty in the reasoning process.

Granted that the propositions of mathematics are necessary for Hume, the next step is to determine whether such propositions are analytic or synthetic. According to Arthur Pap in *Semantics and Necessary Truth,*[4] Hume did not really treat this problem, although logical positivists felt that Hume was the basis of their claim that no *a priori truths* are synthetic. Pap interprets Hume's distinction between relations of ideas and matters of fact to be a distinction between necessary and contingent truths, and, according to Pap, Hume never raised the question whether or not all *a priori truths* are analytic. Pap asks us to consider the following example of Hume's.

3. See *An Enquiry Concerning Human Understanding,* sec. iv, pt. I, p. 22.
4. Arthur Pap, *Semantics and Necessary Truth* (New Haven: Yale University Press, 1958), pp. 69ff.

> In common life 'tis established as a maxim, that the streight-
> est way is always the shortest; which would be as absurd as
> to say, the shortest way is always the shortest, if our idea of
> a right line was not different from that of the shortest way
> betwixt two points.[5]

Hume rejects the claim that "the shortest distance between two
points" is an exact definition of "straight line." Hume says, "I
ask any one, if upon mention of a right line he thinks not
immediately on such a particular appearance, and if 'tis not by
accident only that he considers this property (being the shortest
distance between two points)." [6] Pap claims that Hume is denying that this proposition is analytic. Most important, however, to
Pap's point is the fact that Hume does not deny necessity to this
proposition. Pap's claim is a modest one. Pap argues that Hume
simply "leaves the question open."

Although aspects of logical positivism can be traced to Hume,
there is an important difference about which little has been
made. We have already indicated that Hume valued mathematics as the only discipline in which we preserve a perfect
exactness and certainty. In general, "knowledge," "reason," and
"understanding" were all exclusively concerned with relations of
ideas for Hume. In this sense he certainly followed in the rationalistic tradition of Plato, Descartes, and Leibniz. One can
never be said to have knowledge about matters of fact; one can
only have "belief" or "opinion" about matters of fact. Reason
never operates within the sphere of matters of fact. This reflects
a certain value which Hume placed on the use of the word
"knowledge"— a value which is not shared by the logical positivists. On the contrary, following the tradition of the "revolution
in philosophy," empirically verifiable propositions occupy the
prominent position of being "knowledge." Hume's relations of
ideas have been relegated to the position of being "senseless,"
"trivial," or "giving us no information." The different ways in
which Hume and the logical positivists use the word "knowl-

---

5. D. Hume, *A Treatise of Human Nature,* ed. L. A. Selby-Bigge, Oxford,
1888. Bk. I, pt. II, sec. iv, p. 50.
6. *Ibid.*

edge" indicate the relative importance which relations of ideas (or analytic statements) have to their epistemologies, and where relations of ideas serve as the model of all knowledge and the operating ground for all reason according to Hume, it is matters of fact (affirmed by empirically verifiable statements) which serve in these capacities for the logical positivists.

Hume's treatment of necessity is, unfortunately, heavily laden with psychology in the crucial passages. In his refutation of the claim that "whatever begins to exist, must have a cause of existence" (*Treatise*, Bk. I, pt. III, sec. iii), Hume relies heavily upon conceivability and imagination. The claims of many contemporary philosophers seem to be no less free of psychologism, for example, the claims that an analytic proposition is "self-evident" or "self-explanatory" or "intuitively true." Are not these psychological criteria? How does one determine whether or not x is self-evident? Might it not be self-evident for some and not for others? Are all the truths of mathematics and logic self-evident? Is a lengthy, complicated theorem which follows from a set of axioms only after many manipulations with transformation rules and definitions self-evident? In part, it is the dependence of such attempted drawings of the analytic-synthetic distinction upon psychology which have led to some objections from Quine and White.

KANT

In the Introduction to his *Critique of Pure Reason* Kant makes the distinctions between the two pairs of terms—*a priori, a posteriori* and analytic, synthetic. Kant tells us that *a priori* knowledge is any knowledge which is "independent of experience" and independent of "all impressions of the senses." When Kant says that *a priori* knowledge is that which is "independent of experience," he means "independent of *any* experience whatsoever": "we shall understand *a priori* knowledge, not knowledge independent of this or that experience, but knowledge absolutely independent of all experience." [7] Kant's own example serves suffi-

7. Immanuel Kant, *Critique of Pure Reason*, trans. Norman Kemp Smith (New York: The Macmillan Co., 1963), B 3, p. 43. (B indicates second edition, and A indicates first edition.)

ciently to illustrate his point. If we suppose that a man destroys the foundations of his house, might we not say that he knows *a priori* that it will fall? He does not have to wait upon the house to fall or actually see it fall or even know of its falling to know that destroying the foundations of the house would cause it to fall. But one cannot know that this will happen strictly *a priori* according to Kant because one has first to learn *by experience* things like the law of gravity and that bodies require some sort of support to prevent their falling.

The important question remains, however, of just what Kant means by saying that *a priori* knowledge is that which is "independent of all experience." Kant's position is cloaked in his well-known maxim, ". . . though all our knowledge begins with experience, it does not follow that it all arises out of experience." [8] The first part of this claim is as good a statement as can be found of the position of concept empiricism: one cannot gain knowledge temporally prior to experience. In this sense, then all of our knowledge "begins with experience." Kant intends to emphasize, however, that the origin of our concepts has nothing to do with what is required for *verification*. Thus, he claims that all of our knowledge does not "arise out of experience." An accurate paraphrase of this claim is, "All of our knowledge need not be verified by reference to sense experience." This clearly categorizes Kant as a verification rationalist. Consider Kant's example, '7 + 5 = 12.' Kant would readily admit that experience is necessary to master the concepts '7,' '+,' '5,' '=,' and '12.' One must learn by experience what these concepts mean, but one need not rely upon experience to judge the truth of '7 + 5 = 12'; this is done "independent of all experience."

Kant recognizes that what is needed is a criterion by which to distinguish with certainty between pure (*a priori*) and empirical (*a posteriori*) knowledge. Kant actually gives two such criteria. He says, "if we have a proposition which in being thought is thought as necessary it is an *a priori* judgment; and if, besides, it is not derived from any proposition except one which has the validity of a necessary judgment, it is an absolutely *a priori* judgment." [9] Kant can be interpreted as saying that for any x (where

8. *Ibid.*, B 1, p. 41.
9. *Ibid.*, B 3, p. 43.

x ranges over the class of judgments), x is *a priori* if x is necessary or if x follows by strict deduction from and only from
necessary judgments. It would certainly be objected by the contemporary philosophers who reject the analytic-synthetic distinction that Kant has only "shifted ground"—that he has found his
criterion only by raising another problem. Quine and White
would surely ask, "Are we not left with the problem of determining what 'necessary' means?"

Another criterion offered by Kant to determine *a priori* knowledge is strict universality. He says that when "a judgment is
thought with strict universality, that is, in such a manner that no
exception is allowed as possible, it is not derived from experience, but is valid absolutely *a priori*." [10] It is important to point
out that by "strict universality" Kant did not mean the universality which is characteristic of inductive generalizations, for example, All bodies are heavy. This kind of universality is called
"empirical universality" by Kant because it is simply a generalization from a principle holding in some cases to one which
holds in all. In strict universality, there is no logical possibility
of an exception. Actually, these two criteria of *a priori* knowledge can be interpreted as one because if "x has strict universality" is interpreted as making any exception to x logically
impossible, then this is the same as saying "x is necessary."

It is interesting to compare the thoughts of the empiricists
and Kant on necessity and strict universality, and to notice how
the basic presuppositions of each decided respectively their conclusions. The empiricists carefully inspect all of experience to
try to find from where the notions of necessity and strict universality come. They find none. Consequently, they conclude, on
the basis of empiricist premises, that such notions are illusory and
are really nothing but the propensity of the mind to operate in a
certain way. Kant, seeking the justification of necessity and strict
universality, examines experience. Because he found no justification in experience Kant concluded that necessity and strict
universality cannot characterize empirical (*a posteriori*) knowledge, they must characterize necessary (*a priori*) knowledge. The

10. *Ibid.*, B 4, p. 44.

empiricists' conclusion follows from their assumption that if x cannot be verified by an appeal to experience then it cannot be verified at all. This might well be called the *a priori* assumption of empiricism. Kant's conclusion follows from his basic rationalistic assumption that necessity and strict universality can be justified; so if they cannot be justified *a posteriori*, they must be justified *a priori*.

Kant's second distinction is between analytic and synthetic judgments. It is appropriate to speak of *a priori* and *a posteriori* knowledge and analytic and synthetic judgments or propositions because the former distinction is one regarding methods of verification, and the analytic-synthetic distinction is one which depends on the semantical and syntactical relationships between the terms or symbols of judgments (or propositions).

Kant tells us that in all judgments the relationship between the subject and predicate can be one of two. Either the predicate belongs to the subject, or the predicate does not belong to the subject. In the former case the judgment is analytic, and in the latter it is synthetic. Actually, Kant gives three characteristics of analytic propositions. Analytic propositions for Kant are (1) those in which the predicate is "contained in" the subject; (2) those in which the connection between subject and predicate is one of identity; (3) those which one cannot deny without being involved in a self-contradiction. Of course, synthetic propositions for Kant are (1) those in which the predicate "lies outside" the subject; (2) those in which the connection between subject and predicate is not one of identity; (3) those which one can deny without being involved in a self-contradiction. "All bodies are extended" is an example of an analytic judgment according to Kant, and "All bodies are heavy" is synthetic.

Kant's description of analytic statements as ones in which the predicate is "contained in" the subject involves a major difficulty. Kant's use of "contained in" leaves the problem hopelessly on the metaphorical level. In regards to Kant's other criteria of analytic judgments—that the connection between subject and predicate is one of identity and that one cannot deny analytic judgments without being involved in a self-contradiction—it is interesting that both identity and self-contradictoriness are among those concepts which Quine claims are as much in need of elucidation as is analyticity.

We have seen earlier that in synthetic judgments Kant has said that the predicates lie outside the subjects, that is, they are not connected by identity. What then is the nature of the connections between subjects and predicates in synthetic judgments? If these connections are given in experience (and, consequently, are contingent), then the judgments are *a posteriori*. Consider again, "All bodies are heavy." This judgment is synthetic for Kant because 'heavy' is, in no way, "contained in" 'bodies.' The connection between 'bodies' and 'heavy' is derived from experience and is contingent, and the universality indicated by "all" is empirical universality and not strict universality. Such a connection yields a synthetic *a posteriori* judgment.

Kant devotes his first *Critique* to answering the question, "How are synthetic *a priori* judgments possible?" Basically, Kant was considering the same epistemological problem treated by Hume and the other empiricists. He wanted to justify necessity and strict universality, but he could not do this by an appeal to experience. Where the empiricists were willing to give up necessity and strict universality, Kant was not; however, he could not claim that our knowledge of these concepts depends solely upon the "conformity of the mind to its objects." This is evident because if knoweldge depends solely upon the "conformity of the mind to its objects" and if there cannot be found "necessary connections" in these objects, how does one explain the possibility of making judgments which are necessary and strictly universal? It is this problem which led Kant to his "Copernican revolution" by which he tries to justify synthetic *a priori* judgments as necessary presuppositions for experience. Knowledge does not consist in the "conformity of the mind to its objects" but in the conformity of objects to certain *a priori* categories.

The degree to which the revolution succeeds is directly proportional to the degree to which Kant's distinctions between *a priori* and *a posteriori* knowledge and analytic and synthetic statements can be defended. Kant's treatments of mathematics, pure geometry, physics, and ethics all hinge upon these distinctions. Also, the epistemologies of most post-Kantian philosophers (with the exceptions of Hegel and his followers) similarly hinge upon these distinctions. This holds equally well for those philosophers who agree with Kant regarding synthetic *a priori* judgments and those philosophers who disagree with Kant and argue so strongly against him, for example, Ayer and Wittgenstein.

## CONTEMPORARY PHILOSOPHY

The supposed distinction between analytic statements and synthetic statements has also figured largely in more recent philosophical work. Perhaps the most instructive way to indicate this is to rehearse what may well be the most striking philosophical development of the present century: the attempt to do away finally with metaphysics. Whether this attempt is viewed as euthanasia or regicide, there is no question as to its importance, and no doubt about the deep involvement of the putative distinction between analytic and synthetic. Hence, the importance of the distinction itself.

Roughly sketched, the background is as follows: In relatively remote tradition lie some of the forces to be mustered for the attack upon metaphysics, and the most natural point of historical focus is classical empiricism. For the sake of avoiding needless excursions into texts and frustration over the particular differences between particular empiricists, let us consider Everyman's Empiricist, a convenient device for summarizing the relevant empiricist doctrines.

According to our Everyman's Empiricist (now speaking with a contemporary tongue) all statements may be divided into two kinds. On the one hand, there are those which are necessarily true or necessarily false, and on the other there are those which, though true or false, are not necessarily so. The former are to be called "analytic," the latter, "synthetic." (It goes without saying that our Everyman's Empiricist is no reporter, and produces the structure of the argument rather than a literal representation of classical empiricism.) Analytic sentences, being either necessarily true or necessarily false, are such that no extra-linguistic states of affairs could affect their truth or falsity. No possible meteorological conditions, for example, could affect the truth of

'Either it is snowing or it is not' (suitably qualified as to place and time); it remains true no matter what. Likewise, 'It is both snowing and not snowing' is doomed to falsity no matter what the weather is like. But, so the argument goes, if analytic sentences are immune to worldly states of affairs, local or remote, they can hardly be supposed to deal in worldly states of affairs at all: if no possible meteorological condition could affect the truth of 'Either it is snowing or it is not,' then it can hardly have anything to do with the weather. 'It is both snowing and not snowing' has no meteorological import just because no possible condition could render it true. And so it goes for analytic sentences generally; they owe their truth or falsity to meaning rather than to fact.

There is one possible blemish in Everyman's Empiricist's account so far. It lies in the over-hasty conclusion that analytic statements have nothing to do with states of affairs. For, although analytic statements may have nothing to do with meteorological or other such states of affairs, they nonetheless deal with a class of special states of affairs, namely relations of ideas. But our Everyman's Empiricist is not to be too severely chidden for diverging from classical empiricism. The view that analytic statements traffic in inward rather than outward states of affairs is simply a version of a general thesis; another version is that analytic statements deal solely with language. For the purposes at hand we may supply Everyman's Empiricist with a rider to the effect that while analytic statements may seem to have commerce in extra-mental or extra-linguistic states of affairs, they really do not. They do not have to do with those states of affairs which, on the surface, are their business. 'Either it is snowing or it is not' seems to be about the weather, but really it has to do with ideas, especially those expressed by 'or' and 'not,' or with the words themselves.

Synthetic statements, on the other hand, most emphatically have to do with worldly states of affairs, the more local, the better, because of handiness to observation. Given linguistic constancy, the truth or falsity of synthetic statements depends wholly upon worldly states of affairs. Synthetic statements are thus contingent—at the mercy of states of affairs. Indeed, they are doubly vulnerable in a way in which analytic statements are not. For although analytic statements may possibly have their truth or falsity affected by linguistic change, synthetic statements may be affected either by it or by the relevant facts. Thus, although 'A rose is a rose' is immune to any botanical facts, its truth would nonetheless be affected by the passing of a deadline after which 'rose' was to have the sense of 'turtle,' provided that the deadline occurred sometime between the two occurrences of 'rose' therein. On the other hand, 'Roses are red' is vulnerable both to linguistic change and to the color of roses. Synthetic statements are therefore more risky than analytic statements. The contingency of synthetic statements is one of the articles upon which the anti-metaphysical argument trades.

Thus, the distinction between necessity and contingency evolves into a distinction between unworldliness and worldliness, and there emerges the view that analytic statements have nothing to do with the extra-linguistic (and/or extra-mental) world, while synthetic statements are wholly vulnerable to its states of affairs. Then our Everyman's Empiricist adds the predictable garnish. Sentences having to do with worldly states of affairs, that is, synthetic statements having to do with extra-linguistic facts, are all connected to observation, direct or indirect. What we know about worldly states of affairs, we know by means of observation. This dose of empiricism can be administered in different strengths, but comes as no surprise. In any case, synthetic and, therefore, worldly sentences are tied to observation.

It is easy to see how these materials could be exploited in a general attack upon metaphysics. For according to our Everyman's Empiricist, metaphysical claims pretend to be both necessary and worldly at once. Thus construed, metaphysical claims fare badly at the hands of Everyman's Empiricist, because worldly claims are synthetic and necessary claims are unworldly, and metaphysicians which are the quarry of Everyman's Empiricist maintain that their claims are both worldly and necessarily true. No metaphysician worth his salt, the Empiricist would argue, could admit that his lush theories were concerned only with words or ideas. Likewise, no metaphysician could admit that those theories were merely contingent. And lastly, no metaphysician could admit that his claims about the world resulted from so untrustworthy a process as sensory observation. Thus, the distinction between analytic statements and synthetic statements leaves no place for the metaphysician's claims and constitutes a launching point for an assault upon traditional metaphysics. And the very possibility of drawing the distinction emerges as crucially important.

It should not go unremarked that our Empiricist is scouting Rationalists here and not metaphysicians generally. He views Rationalists as making claims about the world which are supposed to be necessarily true and independent of observation. But Descartes' dream of a physics possessed of the certainty of mathematics is for our Everyman's Empiricist a fairy tale. And the notion that knowledge of the outside world can be attained innately or by intuition is superstition. Synthetic sentences are the ones which have to do with the outside world, and they are both contingent and tied to observation. On two counts, then, the Rationalist's claims about the world fail. Indeed, it may well be that the most illuminating way of conceiving empiricism is through its tacit denial of the possibility of synthetic *a priori* knowledge of the world.

In any case, our Everyman's Empiricist should not be thought of as assaulting metaphysics in general but rather the Rationalists in particular. And this with good reason: for construing necessary truths and falsehoods as having to do exclusively with words or ideas may well be viewed as a metaphysical claim. Indeed, it is worth inquiring whether the empiricist apparatus itself can be justified on empiricist grounds. But that is a tale for another time.

So much for the fable of Everyman's Empiricist. What should be noted in passing is that there appear to be some gaps in his argument. The first is between the claim that analytic statements are unaffected by any states of affairs (save linguistic ones and possibly those involving ideas), and the claim that analytic statements have nothing to do with worldly states of affairs. *Non sequitur* haunts this move. It may well be that 'Either it is snowing or it is not' cannot be affected by any local weather conditions, but it does follow that it has nothing to do with the weather. It might, in fact, be construed as heralding a ubiquitous meteorological condition. The necessary truths of mathematics have sometimes been construed as having to do with numbers, or with classes.

It is instructive to note that the case for factual emptiness appears to be better made with respect to necessarily false statements. For, it might be argued, necessary falsehoods could hardly answer to any states of affairs at all. But this argument trades on the contrast between necessary truths and necessary falsehoods, and hence its extension to necessary truths is unlikely.

There is another gap between the claim that synthetic statements have to do with worldly states of affairs and the claim that they must be tied to observation. Indeed, the requirement that any synthetic statement must ultimately be capable of being checked by observation is no innocent and obvious qualification. It is, in fact, a principal shibboleth of empiricism, which ranges close to being a dogma. Of course traditional empiricism might allow synthetic sentences about ideas, these latter presumably being unobservable. But rather than being noteworthy exceptions to our recent representations, such sentences are the source of much mischief for the empiricist. On empiricist grounds how is discourse about ideas to be justified at all? Whence came the empiricist's idea of an idea? And what sense could be made of the supposition that ideas were, after all, observable? These questions may prove to be of some difficulty for the empiricist, but they need not detain us. It is worth noting, however, that ideas have come to occupy an increasingly less important position in empiricist theory.

However the case of Everyman's Empiricist is to be disposed of, his argument depends upon the possibility of drawing a clear distinction between analytic and synthetic statements. Lacking that distinction, his argument concerning worldliness and unworldliness evaporates, and, among other results, the consigning of certain books to the flames ought to be postponed, if only temporarily.

Everyman's Empiricist was a fiction invented for sake of convenience and brevity. But the Wittgenstein of the *Tractatus* actually deployed these resources against traditional metaphysics. Although the result was self-immolation, the assault was nonetheless important news. The fable of Everyman's Empiricist facilitates our description of Wittgenstein's attack. The action was roughly as follows: Possible statements are of two kinds, those which are tautologies, and those which are not. Those which are tautologies are either necessarily true or necessarily false. Tautologies, therefore, are factually empty (for familiar reasons), while on the other hand those statements which have factual content are contingent. The price of necessity is thus factual content, while the price of factual content is necessity. And the metaphysicians who supposed their claims to be both necessary and factual are undercut because they cannot make a statement. There are no statements of the kind they wish to make. The best they can do is to make what appear to them to be claims about the world, but which really are not. They are not statements at all. With Wittgenstein, as with his intellectual forebears, contingent factuality was tied to observation; observation is ultimately necessary to ascertain the truth or falsity of factual statements. But matters requiring observation, empirical matters, are not the proper business of the philosopher at all. Metaphysical statements are *ersatz* statements, outside the realm of real statements. Metaphysicians thus only appear to produce theories about the world when actually there can be no such theories. Indeed, philosophy should not be thought of as the constructing of theories at all. Rather, it is the activity of clarifying language.

The foregoing reconstruction of the argument of the *Tractatus* shows that, despite its apparent innocence—due, perhaps, to the fact that it has to do with language rather than hardware—the supposed distinction between analytic statements and synthetic statements can have radical consequences. It is clear that this total rejection of metaphysics depends upon the distinction.

It is no news that the striking thing about the *Tractatus* is its self-destructiveness. For the sentences which express its central doctrines turn out not to be statements at all, because they are neither empirically factual nor tautological. Its author recognized this, and speaking of it, used the famous metaphor of the ladder. Playing on the metaphor, it is to be wondered how the ladder could have been climbed in the first place if it is to be cast away as unreal. Important nonsense is nonetheless nonsense, and the *Tractatus* jeopardizes itself in a way too serious to be dismissed by a metaphor. To pursue the *Tractatus* further, however, would deflect us from our purpose. It is enough to note that once again the attack on metaphysics has depended upon the supposed distinction.

The final case is that of Logical Positivism. The positivists were perhaps the most vocal opponents of metaphysics. In an age of enormous advances in the sciences, philosophers found themselves still debating the same old problems, and this suggested that one possible diagnosis was that what they were trying to do could not be done. With the positivists, this took the form of claiming that while metaphysicians thought they were producing meaningful theories about the world, what they were in fact producing was nonsense. In this last, the positivists went a step beyond the *Tractatus*. The positivist attack on metaphysics thus turned upon its criterion of meaningfulness. Cognitively meaningful statements are two kinds: those which are logically true or logically false, and those which are not only contingent, but are also, in principle, verifiable by observation. These two are the familiar analytic and synthetic. All other purported statements are cognitively meaningless. But metaphysical statements are neither logically true or logically false nor verifiable in principle, and hence, they are cognitively meaningless. Thus, metaphysics is to be dismissed. The connection of this argument with classical empiricism and with the *Tractatus* is obvious. And the progression from the fictitious empiricist's unworldliness through Wittgenstein's lack of statementhood to the positivists's meaninglessness is neither surprising nor unnatural.

With respect to the positivist's actual argument, one query that suggests itself is why metaphysical statements must be neither logically true nor logically false. Presumably the answer is that, if they were logically true or logically false, they would be invulnerable to the way the world is, while they are intended to report the way the world is. The contingency of metaphysical statements is thus viewed as a consequence of their worldiness. So once again, the strategy depends upon the drawing of a distinction between analytic statements and synthetic statements.

By way of summary, we have indicated the role of the supposed distinction between analytic and synthetic statements in the recent attacks on traditional metaphysics. This distinction appears to be essential to classical empiricism, as well as necessary for a certain kind of attack on metaphysics. Supposing that Quine and others have at least temporarily unhorsed the latter-day assailants of traditional metaphysics, are we then to suppose that he is a champion of all that Wittgenstein and the positivists thought was nonsense? Is Quine, in other words, the apostle of the sort of philosophy which immediately preceded the twentieth century? The answer would seem to be a ringing negative. As will be seen in "Two Dogmas of Empiricism," the reformed empiricism envisioned by Quine is no safe haven for the views against which Wittgenstein and the positivists were inveighing.

It is not to be wondered, then, that challenges to the distinction by eminent philosophers should provoke a considerable response. "Two Dogmas of Empiricism" is one of the vehicles of that challenge, and is justly celebrated. Since it seems to have provoked the most substantial critical response, it behooves us to begin with it.

# TWO DOGMAS OF EMPIRICISM

## W. V. Quine

*Quine distinguishes between two kinds of supposed analytic statements: those which are logically true (or true by virtue of their form alone) and those which are true by virtue of meaning, not logically true but true because of their nonlogical content. The first kind invariably remain true under any uniform substitution for their nonlogical expressions. For example, 'Every rose is a rose' remains true when 'turtle' is substituted for 'rose' therein. Logical truths are truths which retain their truth no matter what systematic substitution is made for their nonlogical terms. On the other hand, the latter kind cannot be characterized so easily. Thus, although 'No bachelor is married' (which is not a logical truth, not true by virtue of its form alone) can be made into a logical truth by substituting 'unmarried person' for*

From *The Philosophical Review*, vol. 60, 1951. Reprinted by permission of *The Philosophical Review* and the author.

'bachelor' on the basis of their purported synonymy, the matter is not closed. For the notion of synonymy is every bit as mysterious as is the notion of analyticity. Characterization of the second class of analytic statements failing thus, the notion of analyticity itself remains incompletely analyzed.

Carnap's notion of state descriptions is of no help. For if the language with respect to which 'analytic' is to be defined is rich enough to contain orthographically dissimilar synonyms, then the statements of the second kind would become synthetic, a far cry from being satisfactorily classified as analytic.

Likewise, definition does not clarify the putative analyticity of statements of the second kind. For, except for stipulative definitions whereby synonymy is achieved by more or less arbitrary fiat, definitions are best viewed as reports of pre-existing synonymies. And thus, analyticity once again depends upon the equally obscure notion of synonymy.

Pursuing, then, the notion of synonymy in the interests of capturing the notion of analyticity, the suggestion that synonymy consists in interchangeability is entertained. If the notion of analyticity is assumed to be antecedently in hand, then the synonymy of two expressions, 'A' and 'B' can be treated as the analyticity of 'All and only A are B.' But since the idea is to get ultimately at the notion of analyticity, this course is of no avail. It can be shown, however, that interchangeability does yield synonymy. From the interchangeability of 'A' and 'B' and the evident truth 'Necessarily all and only A are A,' there emerges, by dint of substitution, 'Necessarily all and only A are B,' which ultimately implies that 'A' and 'B' are synonymous. But this account will satisfy only if 'necessarily' yields a truth only when prefixed to an analytic statement. Thus, the notion of analyticity is once again presupposed rather than explained.

For extensional languages, interchangeability does not guarantee synonymy, sameness of extension not being sameness of meaning, while languages containing 'necessarily,' as recently construed, presuppose analyticity.

This result prompts the reflection that the right strategy may be to attack analyticity first, and then proceed to synonymy. It *might be thought that analyticity could be satisfactorily char-acterized by appealing to the semantical rules of an artificial lan-guage. But semantical rules which explicitly characterize certain statements as analytic are of no help, presupposing, as they do, an antecedently intelligible notion of analyticity. Semantical rules which segregate a certain segment of truths (which are to be called "analytic" because of their accord with the rules), which avoid the epithet "analytic," are likewise inutile, because not all truths are to be regarded as analytic, and the notion of semantical rule then inherits all of the obscurity featured by the notion of analyticity. The purported distinction between analytic and synthetic remains shrouded; the supposition that there is such a distinction remains a dogma.*

*Quine then takes up the verification theory of meaning, ac-cording to which statements are synonymous when and only when the way of verifying each is the same. Reductionism re-quires the construal of all statements as translatable into state-ments about immediate experience. Such is the relation between a statement and its verifying experiences. But reduction-ism is itself a dogma: rather than the translation of statements singly, the fact is that statements are collectively tested by experience.*

*Indeed, the two dogmas come to the same thing: they suppose a distinction between that which has to do with experience and that which has to do with language alone (or between worldli-ness and unworldliness). Total science is an interrelated whole, parts of which are more directly affected by experience than others. But every part is, to one degree or another, vulnerable to alteration as need arises. And any alteration of our conceptual scheme is "where rational, pragmatic."*

*Some points worth pondering with respect to "Two Dogmas of Empiricism" are as follows. In the initial exposition (Section I) it is supposed that a class of logical expressions such as 'no,' 'un-,' 'if,' and so on, can be segregated for future purposes. But it may be wondered whether such expressions in fact enjoy sanc-tuary from the general action against analyticity. How are such expressions identified as logical expressions? Is the putative synonymy of 'not' and 'un-' not involved? It is clear that the verdict that these are truth-functionally identical depends upon their prior synonymy. For how else could one assign the same truth values to 'x is not married' and 'x is unmarried?' The intriguing thing is that, if the logical expressions cannot be segregated without considerations of synonymy, thus dampening the original argument, there nonetheless may emerge an even stronger argument against the distinction. For the effect would be to undermine the distinction between the two classes of purportedly analytical statements, thus perhaps making them both subject to Quine's strictures.*

*There is, further, a scruple to be encountered concerning the open-ended nature of Quine's argument. For although he has canvassed the most natural possibilities for drawing the distinction, he has, presumably, not canvassed them all. It would be picky in the extreme, of course, to point out that from the failure of the alternatives he selects, it does not follow that there is no distinction to be drawn. But it is not necessarily nit-picking to suggest that there are possibilities which have at least the hint of promise. For example, it might be possible to characterize synthetic statements, perhaps in terms of observation or factual content, thus isolating the analytic statements by process of elimination.*

*Another interesting question is whether there is anything left of empiricism once the two dogmas have been exorcised. For it is not merely a question of clinging to the view that we acquire our knowledge of the world around us by means of observation. It would be extremely difficult to find a (sane) rationalist dogged enough to deny that the handiest way to find out whether there are rats in the cellar is to go down and look. But we shall see that Quine seems to consider that empiricism can survive without the dogmas. (It may not be necessary to remind the reader that the extreme danger of attributing anything to anybody is what necessitates the cowardly language exemplified by 'seems to consider.' Maybe if we made mistaken attribution a less dire sin, we could use bolder language.) The great rationalists sought, in one way or another, to achieve for science the certainty possessed by mathematics, if we may indulge ourselves just for a moment with broad (and undocumented) historical speculation.*

*What corresponded to this quest in classical empiricism was the second of the dogmas attacked by Quine: the notion that all of our knowledge of the world around us had to be reducible to direct experience. Reduction to direct experience was to the empiricist what the bestowal of the certainty of mathematics was to the rationalist. Quine, as we shall see, regards the notion of such reduction as a dogma. And if the empiricist attitude about the relation of experience to knowledge about the world can be put in terms of such reduction (and if our penny historical speculations are correct), then there is no empiricism without the dogmas. Whether it should be mourned is another question completely.*

*Lastly, another course would be to exclude the statements of the second class (those which are purportedly analytic, but are not logical truths) from the class of analytic statements. Quine is not, after all, protesting a certain class of statements, but rather the distinction itself. Drawing it differently, namely, counting only logical truths as analytic, may provide a satisfactory way of drawing it. If so, the conclusions drawn from the failure of the distinction are in jeopardy.*

*These latter suggestions have been intended as stimuli rather than as polemics; whither they lead remains to be seen.*

Modern empiricism has been conditioned in large part by two dogmas. One is a belief in some fundamental cleavage between truths which are *analytic,* or grounded in meanings independently of matters of fact, and truths which are *synthetic,* or grounded in fact. The other dogma is *reductionism*: the belief that each meaningful statement is equivalent to some logical construct upon terms which refer to immediate experience. Both dogmas, I shall argue, are ill founded. One effect of abandoning them is, as we shall see, a blurring of the supposed boundary between speculative metaphysics and natural science. Another effect is a shift toward pragmatism.

### 1. BACKGROUND FOR ANALYTICITY

Kant's cleavage between analytic and synthetic truths was fore-shadowed in Hume's distinction between relations of ideas and matters of fact, and in Leibniz's distinction between truths of reason and truths of fact. Leibniz spoke of the truths of reason as true in all possible worlds. Picturesqueness aside, this is to say that the truths of reason are those which could not possibly be false. In the same vein we hear analytic statements defined as statements whose denials are self-contradictory. But this defi-nition has small explanatory value; for the notion of self-contradictoriness, in the quite broad sense needed for this defini-tion of analyticity, stands in exactly the same need of clarifica-tion as does the notion of analyticity itself.[1] The two notions are the two sides of a single dubious coin.

Kant conceived of an analytic statement as one that attributes to its subject no more than is already conceptually contained in the subject. This formulation has two shortcomings: it limits itself to statements of subject-predicate form, and it appeals to a notion of containment which is left at a metaphorical level. But Kant's intent, evident more from the use he makes of the notion of analyticity than from his definition of it, can be re-stated thus: a statement is analytic when it is true by virtue of meanings and independently of fact. Pursuing this line, let us examine the concept of *meaning* which is presupposed.

We must observe to begin with that meaning is not to be identified with naming, or reference. Consider Frege's example of 'Evening Star' and 'Morning Star.' Understood not merely as a recurrent evening apparition but as a body, the Evening Star is the planet Venus, and the Morning Star is the same. The two singular terms *name* the same thing. But the meanings must be treated as distinct, since the identity 'Evening Star = Morn-ing Star' is a statement of fact established by astronomical ob-servation. If 'Evening Star' and 'Morning Star' were alike in

1. See White, "The Analytic and the Synthetic: An Untenable Dualism," *John Dewey: Philosopher of Science and Freedom* (New York, 1950), p. 324.

meaning, the identity 'Evening Star = Morning Star' would be analytic.

Again there is Russel's example of 'Scott' and 'the author of *Waverly*.' Analysis of the meanings of words was by no means sufficient to reveal to George IV that the person named by these two singular terms was one and the same.

The distinction between meaning and naming is no less important at the level of abstract terms. The terms '9' and 'the number of planets' name one and the same abstract entity but presumably must be regarded as unlike in meaning; for astronomical observation was needed, and not mere reflection on meanings, to determine the sameness of the entity in question.

Thus far we have been considering singular terms. With general terms, or predicates, the situation is somewhat different but parallel. Whereas a singular term purports to name an entity, abstract or concrete, a general term does not; but a general term is *true of* an entity, or of each of many, or of none. The class of all entities of which a general term is true is called the *extension* of the term. Now paralleling the contrast between the meaning of a singular term and the entity named, we must distinguish equally between the meaning of a general term and its extension. The general terms 'creature with a heart' and 'creature with a kidney,' e.g., are perhaps alike in extension but unlike in meaning.

Confusion of meaning with extension, in the case of general terms, is less common than confusion of meaning with naming in the case of singular terms. It is indeed a commonplace in philosophy to oppose intention (or meaning) to extension, or, in a variant vocabulary, connotation to denotation.

The Aristotelian notion of essence was the forerunner, no doubt, of the modern notion of intension or meaning. For Aristotle it was essential in men to be rational, accidental to be two-legged. But there is an important difference between this attitude and the doctrine of meaning. From the latter point of view it may indeed be conceded (if only for the sake of argument) that rationality is involved in the meaning of the word 'man' while two-leggedness is not; but two-leggedness may at the same time be viewed as involved in the meaning of 'biped' while rationality is not. Thus from the point of view of the doctrine of meaning it makes no sense to say of the actual individual, who is at once a man and a biped, that his rationality is essential and his two-leggedness accidental or vice versa. Things had essences, for Aristotle, but only linguistic forms have meanings. Meaning is what essence becomes when it is divorced from the object of reference and wedded to the word.

For the theory of meaning the most conspicuous question is as to the nature of its objects: what sort of things are meanings? They are evidently intended to be ideas, somehow—mental ideas for some semanticists, Platonic ideas for others. Objects of either sort are so elusive, not to say debatable, that there seems little hope of erecting a fruitful science about them. It is not even clear, granted meanings, when we have two and when we have one; it is not clear when linguistic forms should be regarded as *synonymous,* or alike in meaning, and when they should not. If a standard of synonymy should be arrived at, we may reasonably expect that the appeal to meanings as entities will not have played a very useful part in the enterprise.

A felt need for meant entities may derive from an earlier failure to appreciate that meaning and reference are distinct. Once the theory of meaning is sharply separated from the theory of reference, it is a short step to recognizing as the business of the theory of meaning simply the synonymy of linguistic forms and the analyticity of statements; meanings themselves, as obscure intermediary entities, may well be abandoned.

The description of analyticity as truth by virtue of meanings started us off in pursuit of a concept of meaning. But now we have abandoned the thought of any special realm of entities called meanings. So the problem of analyticity confronts us anew.

Statements which are analytic by general philosophical acclaim are not, indeed, far to seek. They fall into two classes. Those of the first class, which may be called *logically true,* are typified by:

(1) No unmarried man is married.

The relevant feature of this example is that it is not merely true as it stands, but remains true under any and all reinterpretations of 'man' and 'married.' If we suppose a prior inventory of *logical* particles, comprising 'no,' 'un-' 'if,' 'then,' 'and,' etc., then in general a logical truth is a statement which is true and remains true under all reinterpretations of its components other than the logical particles.

But there is also a second class of analytic statements, typified by:

(2) No bachelor is married.

The characteristic of such a statement is that it can be turned into a logical truth by putting synonyms for synonyms; thus (2) can be turned into (1) by putting 'unmarried man' for its synonym 'bachelor.' We still lack a proper characterization of this second class of analytic statements, and therewith of analyticity generally, inasmuch as we have had in the above description to lean on a notion of 'synonymy' which is no less in need of clarification than analyticity itself.

In recent years Carnap has tended to explain analyticity by appeal to what he calls state-descriptions.[2] A state-description is any exhaustive assignment of truth values to the atomic, or noncompound, statements of the language. All other statements of the language are, Carnap assumes, built up of their component clauses by means of the familiar logical devices, in such a way that the truth value of any complex statement is fixed for each state-description by specifiable logical laws. A statement is then explained as analytic when it comes out true under every state-description. This account is an adaptation of Leibniz's "true in all possible worlds." But note that this version of analyticity serves its purpose only if the atomic statements of the language are, unlike 'John is a bachelor' and 'John is married,' mutually independent. Otherwise there would be a state-description which assigned truth to 'John is a bachelor' and falsity to 'John is married,' and consequently 'All bachelors are married' would turn out synthetic rather than analytic under the proposed criterion. Thus the criterion of analyticity in terms of state-descriptions serves only for languages devoid of extralogical synonym-pairs, such as 'bachelor' and 'unmarried

2. R. Carnap, *Meaning and Necessity* (Chicago, 1947), pp. 9 ff.; *Logical Foundations of Probability* (Chicago, 1950), pp. 70 ff.

man': synonym-pairs of the type which give rise to the "second class" of analytic statements. The criterion in terms of state-descriptions is a reconstruction at best of logical truth.

I do not mean to suggest that Carnap is under any illusions on this point. His simplified model language with its state-descriptions is aimed primarily not at the general problem of analyticity but at another purpose, the clarification of probability and induction. Our problem, however, is analyticity; and here the major difficulty lies not in the first class of analytic statements, the logical truths, but rather in the second class, which depends on the notion of synonymy.

## II. DEFINITION

There are those who find it soothing to say that the analytic statements of the second class reduce to those of the first class, the logical truths, by *definition;* 'bachelor,' for example, is *defined* as 'unmarried man.' But how do we find that 'bachelor' is defined as 'unmarried man'? Who defined it thus, and when? Are we to appeal to the nearest dictionary, and accept the lexicographer's formulation as law? Clearly this would be to put the cart before the horse. The lexicographer is an empirical scientist, whose business is the recording of antecedent facts; and if he glosses 'bachelor' as 'unmarried man' it is because of his belief that there is a relation of synonymy between these forms, implicit in general or preferred usage prior to his own work. The notion of synonymy presupposed here has still to be clarified, presumably in terms relating to linguistic behavior. Certainly the "definition" which is the lexicographer's report of an observed synonymy cannot be taken as the ground of the synonymy.

Definition is not, indeed, an activity exclusively of philologists. Philosophers and scientists frequently have occasion to "define" a recondite term by paraphrasing it into terms of a more familiar vocabulary. But ordinarily such a definition, like the philologist's, is pure lexicography, affirming a relationship of synonymy antecedent to the exposition in hand.

Just what it means to affirm synonymy, just what the interconnections may be which are necessary and sufficient in order that two linguistic forms be properly describable as synonymous, is far from clear; but, whatever these interconnections may be, ordinarily they are grounded in usage. Definitions reporting selected instances of synonymy come then as reports upon usage.

There is also, however, a variant type of definitional activity which does not limit itself to the reporting of pre-existing synonymies. I have in mind what Carnap calls *explication*—an activity to which philosophers are given, and scientists also in their more philosophical moments. In explication the purpose is not merely to paraphrase the definiendum into an outright synonym, but actually to improve upon the definiendum by refining or supplementing its meaning. But even explication, though not merely reporting a pre-existing synonymy between definiendum and definiens, does rest nevertheless on *other* preexisting synonymies. The matter may be viewed as follows. Any word worth explicating has some contexts which, as wholes, are clear and precise enough to be useful; and the purpose of explication is to preserve the usage of these favored contexts while sharpening the usage of other contexts. In order that a given definition be suitable for purposes of explication, therefore, what is required is not that the definiendum in its antecedent usage be synonymous with the definiens, but just that each of these favored contexts of the definiendum, taken as a whole in its antecedent usage, be synonymous with the corresponding context of the definiens.

Two alternative definientia may be equally appropriate for the purposes of a given task of explication and yet not be synonymous with each other; for they may serve interchangeably within the favored contexts but diverge elsewhere. By cleaving to one of these definientia rather than the other, a definition of explicative kind generates, by fiat, a relationship of synonymy between definiendum and definiens which did not hold before. But such a definition still owes its explicative function, as seen, to pre-existing synonymies.

There does, however, remain still an extreme sort of definition which does not hark back to prior synonymies at all; namely, the

explicitly conventional introduction of novel notations for purposes of sheer abbreviation. Here the definiendum becomes
synonymous with the definiens simply because it has been
created expressly for the purpose of being synonymous with the
definiens. Here we have a really transparent case of synonymy
created by definition; would that all species of synonymy were
as intelligible. For the rest, definition rests on synonymy rather
than explaining it.

The word "definition" has come to have a dangerously reassur-
ing sound, due no doubt to its frequent occurrence in logical
and mathematical writings. We shall do well to digress now into
a brief appraisal of the role of definition in formal work.

In logical and mathematical systems either of two mutually
antagonistic types of economy may be striven for, and each has
its peculiar practical utility. On the one hand we may seek
economy of practical expression: ease and brevity in the statement of multifarious relationships. This sort of economy calls
usually for distinctive concise notations for a wealth of concepts.
Second, however, and oppositely, we may seek economy in
grammar and vocabulary; we may try to find a minimum of
basic concepts such that, once a distinctive notation has been
appropriated to each of them, it becomes possible to express
any desired further concept by mere combination and iteration
of our basic notations. This second sort of economy is imprac-
tical in one way, since a poverty in basic idioms tends to a
necessary lengthening of discourse. But it is practical in another
way: it greatly simplifies theoretical discourse *about* the language, through minimizing the terms and the forms of construction wherein the language consists.

Both sorts of economy, though prima facie incompatible, are
valuable in their separate ways. The custom has consequently
arisen of combining both sorts of economy by forging in effect
two languages, the one a part of the other. The inclusive language, though redundant in grammar and vocabulary, is economical in message lengths, while the part, called *primitive
notation,* is economical in grammar and vocabulary. Whole and
part are correlated by rules of translation whereby each idiom
not in primitive notation is equated to some complex built up

of primitive notation. These rules of translation are the so-called *definitions* which appear in formalized systems. They are best viewed not as adjuncts to one language but as correlations between two languages, the one a part of the other.

But these correlations are not arbitrary. They are supposed to show how the primitive notations can accomplish all purposes, save brevity and convenience, of the redundant language. Hence the definiendum and its definiens may be expected, in each case, to be related in one or another of the three ways lately noted. The definiens may be a faithful paraphrase of the definiendum into the narrower notation, preserving a direct synonymy as of antecedent usage; or the definiens may, in the spirit of explication, improve upon the antecedent usage of the definiendum; or finally, the definiendum may be a newly created notation, newly endowed with meaning here and now.

In formal and informal work alike, thus, we find that definition—except in the extreme case of the explicitly conventional introduction of new notations—hinges on prior relationships of synonymy. Recognizing then that the notion of definition does not hold the key to synonymy and analyticity, let us look further into synonymy and say no more of definition.

### III. INTERCHANGEABILITY

A natural suggestion, deserving close examination, is that the synonymy of two linguistic forms consists simply in their interchangeability in all contexts without change of truth value; interchangeability, in Leibniz's phrase, *salva veritate*. Note that synonyms so conceived need not even be free from vagueness, as long as the vaguenesses match.

But it is not quite true that the synonyms 'bachelor' and 'unmarried man' are everywhere interchangeable *salva veritate*. Truths which become false under substitution of 'unmarried man' for 'bachelor' are easily constructed with help of 'bachelor of arts' or 'bachelor's buttons.' Also with help of quotation, thus:

'Bachelor' has less than ten letters.

Such counterinstances can, however, perhaps be set aside by

treating the phrases 'bachelor of arts' and 'bachelor's buttons' and the quotation ' 'bachelor' ' each as a single indivisible word and then stipulating that the interchangeability *salva veritate* which is to be the touchstone of synonymy is not supposed to apply to fragmentary occurrences inside of a word. This account of synonymy, supposing it acceptable on other counts, has indeed the drawback of appealing to a prior conception of "word" which can be counted on to present difficulties of formulation in its turn. Nevertheless some progress might be claimed in having reduced the problem of synonymy to a problem of word-hood. Let us pursue this line a bit, taking "word" for granted.

The question remains whether interchangeability *salva veritate* (apart from occurrences within words) is a strong enough condition for synonymy, or whether, on the contrary, some non-synonymous expressions might be thus interchangeable. Now let us be clear that we are not concerned here with synonymy in the sense of complete identity in psychological associations or poetic quality; indeed no two expressions are synonymous in such a sense. We are concerned only with what may be called *cognitive synonymy*. Just what this is cannot be said without successfully finishing the present study; but we know something about it from the need which arose for it in connection with analyticity in Section I. The sort of synonymy needed there was merely such that any analytic statement could be turned into a logical truth by putting synonyms for synonyms. Turning the tables and assuming analyticity, indeed, we could explain cognitive synonymy of terms as follows (keeping to the familiar example): to say that 'bachelor' and 'unmarried man' are cognitively synonymous is to say no more nor less than that the statement:

(3) All and only bachelors are unmarried men

is analytic.[3]

3. This is cognitive synonymy in a primary, broad sense. Carnap (*Meaning and Necessity*, pp. 56 ff.) and Lewis (*Analysis of Knowledge and Valuation* [La Salle, Ill., 1946], pp. 83 ff.) have suggested how, once this notion is at hand, a narrower sense of cognitive synonymy which is preferable for some purposes can in turn be derived. But this special ramification of concept-building lies aside from the present purposes and must not be confused with the broad sort of cognitive synonymy here concerned.

What we need is an account of cognitive synonymy not pre-supposing analyticity—if we are to explain analyticity conversely with help of cognitive synonymy as undertaken in Section I. And indeed such an independent account of cognitive synonymy is at present up for consideration, namely, interchangeability *salva veritate* everywhere except within words. The question before us, to resume the thread at last, is whether such inter-changeability is a sufficient condition for cognitive synonymy. We can quickly assure ourselves that it is, by examples of the following sort. The statement:

(4) Necessarily all and only bachelors are bachelors

is evidently true, even supposing 'necessarily' so narrowly con-strued as to be truly applicable only to analytic statements. Then, *if* 'bachelor' and 'unmarried man' are interchangeable *salva veritate,* the result

(5) Necessarily, all and only bachelors are unmarried men

of putting 'unmarried man' for an occurrence of 'bachelor' in (4) must, like (4), be true. But to say that (5) is true is to say that (3) is analytic, and hence that 'bachelor' and 'un-married man' are cognitively synonymous.

Let us see what there is about the above argument that gives it its air of hocus-pocus. The condition of interchangeability *salva veritate* varies in its force with variations in the richness of the language at hand. The above argument supposes we are working with a language rich enough to contain the adverb 'necessarily,' this adverb being so construed as to yield truth when and only when applied to an analytic statement. But can we condone a language which contains such an adverb? Does the adverb really make sense? To suppose that it does is to sup-pose that we have already made satisfactory sense of 'analytic.' Then what are we so hard at work on right now?

Our argument is not flatly circular, but something like it. It has the form, figuratively speaking, of a closed curve in space.

Interchangeability *salva veritate* is meaningless until rela-tivized to a language whose extent is specified in relevant respects. Suppose now we consider a language containing just the following materials. There is an indefinitely large stock of one- and many-place predicates, mostly having to do with extra-logical subject matter. The rest of the language is logical. The atomic sentences consist each of a predicate followed by one or more variables; and the complex sentences are built up of atomic ones by truth functions and quantification. In effect such a language enjoys the benefits also of descriptions and class names and indeed singular terms generally, these being contextually definable in known ways.[4] Such a language can be adequate to classical mathematics and indeed to scientific discourse gener-ally, except in so far as the latter involves debatable devices such as modal adverbs and contrary-to-fact conditionals. Now a language of this type is *extensional,* in this sense: any two predicates which *agree extensionally* (i.e., are true of the same objects) are interchangeable *salva veritate.*

In an extensional language, therefore, interchangeability *salva veritate* is no assurance of cognitive synonymy of the desired type. That 'bachelor' and 'unmarried man' are interchangeable *salva veritate* in an extensional language assures us of no more than that (3) is true. There is no assurance here that the extensional agreement of 'bachelor' and 'unmarried man' rests on meaning rather than merely on accidental matters of fact, as does extensional agreement of 'creature with a heart' and 'crea-ture with a kidney.'

For most purposes extensional agreement is the nearest ap-proximation to synonymy we need care about. But the fact re-mains that extensional agreement falls far short of cognitive synonymy of the type required for explaining analyticity in the manner of Section I. The type of cognitive synonymy required there is such as to equate the synonymy of 'bachelor' and 'un-married man' with the analyticity of (3), not merely with the truth of (3).

So we must recognize that interchangeability *salva veritate,* if construed in relation to an extensional language, is not a suffi-cient condition of cognitive synonymy in the sense needed for

4. See, for example my *Mathematical Logic* (New York, 1940; Cam-bridge, Mass., 1947), sec. 24, 26, 27; or *Methods of Logic* (New York, 1950), sec. 37 ff.

deriving analyticity in the manner of Section I. If a language contains an intensional adverb 'necessarily' in the sense lately noted, or other particles to the same effect, then interchangeability *salva veritate* in such a language does afford a sufficient condition of cognitive synonymy; but such a language is intelligible only if the notion of analyticity is already clearly understood in advance.

The effort to explain cognitive synonymy first, for the sake of deriving analyticity from it afterward as in Section I, is perhaps the wrong approach. Instead we might try explaining analyticity somehow without appeal to cognitive synonymy. Afterward we could doubtless derive cognitive synonymy from analyticity satisfactorily enough if desired. We have seen that cognitive synonymy of 'bachelor' and 'unmarried man' can be explained as analyticity of (3). The same explanation works for any pair of one-place predicates, of course, and it can be extended in obvious fashion to many-place predicates. Other syntactical categories can also be accommodated in fairly parallel fashion. Singular terms may be said to be cognitively synonymous when the statement of identity formed by putting '=' between them is analytic. Statements may be said simply to be cognitively synonymous when their biconditional (the result of joining them by 'if and only if') is analytic.[5] If we care to lump all categories into a single formulation, at the expense of assuming again the notion of "word" which was appealed to early in this section, we can describe any two linguistic forms as cognitively synonymous when the two forms are interchangeable (apart from occurrences within "words") *salva* (no longer *veritate* but) *analyticitate*. Certain technical questions arise, indeed, over cases of ambiguity or homonymy; let us not pause for them, however, for we are already digressing. Let us rather turn our backs on the problem of synonymy and address ourselves anew to that of analyticity.

5. The 'if and only if' itself is intended in the truth functional sense. See Carnap, *Meaning and Necessity,* p. 14.

Analyticity at first seemed most naturally definable by appeal to a realm of meanings. On refinement, the appeal to meanings gave way to an appeal to synonymy or definition. But definition turned out to be a will-o'-the-wisp, and synonymy turned out to be best understood only by dint of a prior appeal to analyticity itself. So we are back at the problem of analyticity.

I do not know whether the statement 'Everything green is extended' is analytic. Now does my indecision over this example really betray an incomplete understanding, an incomplete grasp of the "meanings," of 'green' and 'extended'? I think not. The trouble is not with 'green' or 'extended,' but with 'analytic.'

It is often hinted that the difficulty in separating analytic statements from synthetic ones in ordinary language is due to the vagueness of ordinary language and that the distinction is clear when we have a precise artificial language with explicit "semantical rules." This, however, as I shall now attempt to show, is a confusion.

The notion of analyticity about which we are worrying is a purported relation between statements and languages: a statement $S$ is said to be *analytic for* a language $L$, and the problem is to make sense of this relation generally, for example, for variable '$S$' and '$L$.' The point that I want to make is that the gravity of this problem is not perceptibly less for artificial languages than for natural ones. The problem of making sense of the idiom '$S$ *is analytic for* $L$,' with variable '$S$' and '$L$,' retains its stubbornness even if we limit the range of the variable '$L$' to artificial languages. Let me now try to make this point evident.

For artificial languages and semantical rules we look naturally to the writings of Carnap. His semantical rules take various forms, and to make my point I shall have to distinguish certain of the forms. Let us suppose, to begin with, an artificial language $L_0$ whose semantical rules have the form explicitly of a specification, by recursion or otherwise, of all the analytic statements of $L_0$. The rules tell us that such and such statements, and only those, are the analytic statements of $L_0$. Now here the difficulty is simply that the rules contain the word 'analytic,' which we do not understand! We understand what expressions the rules attribute analyticity to, but we do not understand what the rules attribute to those expressions. In short, before we can understand a rule which begins "A statement S is analytic for language $L_0$ if and only if . . . ," we must understand the general relative term 'analytic for'; we must understand 'S is analytic for $L$' where 'S' and '$L$' are variables.

Alternatively we may, indeed, view the so-called rule as a conventional definition of a new simple symbol 'analytic-for-$L_0$,' which might better be written untendentiously as '$K$' so as not to seem to throw light on the interesting word "analytic." Obviously any number of classes $K, M, N$, etc., of statements of $L_0$ can be specified for various purposes or for no purpose; what does it mean to say that $K$, as against $M, N$, etc., is the class of the 'analytic' statements of $L_0$?

By saying what statements are analytic for $L_0$ we explain 'analytic-for $L_0$' but not 'analytic for.' We do not begin to explain the idiom 'S is analytic for $L$' with variable 'S' and '$L$,' even though we be content to limit the range of '$L$' to the realm of artificial languages.

Actually we do know enough about the intended significance of 'analytic' to know that analytic statements are supposed to be true. Let us then turn to a second form of semantical rule, which says not that such and such statements are analytic but simply that such and such statements are included among the truths. Such a rule is not subject to the criticism of containing the un-understood word 'analytic'; and we may grant for the sake of argument that there is no difficulty over the broader term 'true.' A semantical rule of this second type, a rule of truth, is not supposed to specify all the truths of the language; it merely stipulates, recursively or otherwise, a certain multitude of statements which, along with others unspecified, are to count as true. Such a rule may be conceded to be quite clear. Derivatively, afterward, analyticity can be demarcated thus: a statement is analytic if it is (not merely true but) true according to the semantical rule.

Still there is really no progress. Instead of appealing to an unexplained word 'analytic,' we are now appealing to an unexplained phrase 'semantical rule.' Not every true statement which says that the statements of some class are true can count as a semantical rule—otherwise *all* truths would be "analytic" in the sense of being true according to semantical rules. Semantical rules are distinguishable, apparently, only by the fact of appearing on a page under the heading 'Semantical Rules'; and this heading is itself then meaningless.

We can say indeed that a statement is *analytic-for-$L_0$* if and only if it is true according to such and such specifically appended "semantical rules," but then we find ourselves back at essentially the same case which was originally discussed: '$S$ is analytic-for-$L_0$ if and only if. . . .' Once we seek to explain '$S$ is analytic for $L$' generally for variable '$L$' (even allowing limitation of '$L$' to artificial languages), the explanation 'true according to the semantical rules of $L$' is unavailing; for the relative term 'semantical rule of' is as much in need of clarification, at least, as 'analytic for.'

It might conceivably be protested that an artificial language $L$ (unlike a natural one) is a language in the ordinary sense *plus* a set of explicit semantical rules—the whole constituting, let us say, an ordered pair; and that the semantical rules of $L$ then are specifiable simply as the second component of the pair $L$. But, by the same token and more simply, we might construe an artificial language $L$ outright as an ordered pair whose second component is the class of its analytic statements; and then the analytic statements of $L$ become specifiable simply as the statements in the second component of $L$. Or better still, we might just stop tugging at our bootstraps altogether.

Not all the explanations of analyticity known to Carnap and his readers have been covered explicitly in the above considerations, but the extension to other forms is not hard to see. Just one additional factor should be mentioned which sometimes enters: sometimes the semantical rules are in effect rules of translation into ordinary language, in which case the analytic statements of the artificial language are in effect recognized as such from the analyticity of their specified translations in ordinary language. Here certainly there can be no thought of an illumination of the problem of analyticity from the side of the artificial language.

From the point of view of the problem of analyticity the notion of an artificial language with semantical rules is a *feu follet par excellence*. Semantical rules determining the analytic statements of an artificial language are of interest only in so far as we already understand the notion of analyticity; they are of no help in gaining this understanding.

Appeal to hypothetical languages of an artificially simple kind could conceivably be useful in clarifying analyticity, if the mental or behavioral or cultural factors relevant to analyticity—whatever they may be—were somehow sketched into the simplified model. But a model which takes analyticity merely as an irreducible character is unlikely to throw light on the problem of explicating analyticity.

It is obvious that truth in general depends on both language and extra-linguistic fact. The statement 'Brutus killed Caesar' would be false if the world had been different in certain ways, but it would also be false if the word 'killed' happened rather to have the sense of 'begat.' Hence the temptation to suppose in general that the truth of a statement is somehow analyzable into a linguistic component and a factual component. Given this supposition, it next seems reasonable that in some statements the factual component should be null; and these are the analytic statements. But, for all its *a priori* reasonableness, a boundary between analytic and synthetic statements simply has not been drawn. That there is such a distinction to be drawn at all is an unempirical dogma of empiricists, a metaphysical article of faith.

### V. THE VERIFICATION THEORY AND REDUCTIONISM

In the course of these somber reflections we have taken a dim view first of the notion of meaning, then of the notion of cognitive synonymy, and finally of the notion of analyticity. But what, it may be asked, of the verification theory of meaning? This phrase has established itself so firmly as a catchword of empiricism that we should be very unscientific indeed not to look beneath it for a possible key to the problem of meaning and the associated problems.

The verification theory of meaning, which has been conspicuous in the literature from Peirce onward, is that the meaning of a statement is the method of empirically confirming or infirming it. An analytic statement is that limiting case which is confirmed no matter what.

As urged in Section I, we can as well pass over the question of meanings as entities and move straight to sameness of meaning, or synonymy. Then what the verification theory says is that statements are synonymous if and only if they are alike in point of method of empirical confirmation or infirmation.

This is an account of cognitive synonymy not of linguistic forms generally, but of statements.[6] However, from the concept of synonymy of statements we could derive the concept of synonymy for other linguistic forms, by considerations somewhat similar to those at the end of Section III. Assuming the notion of "word," indeed, we could explain any two forms as synonymous when the putting of the one form for an occurrence of the other in any statement (apart from occurrences within "words") yields a synonymous statement. Finally, given the concept of synonymy thus for linguistic forms generally, we could define analyticity in terms of synonymy and logical truth as in Section I. For that matter, we could define analyticity more simply in terms of just synonymy of statements together with logical truth; it is not necessary to appeal to synonymy of linguistic forms other than statements. For a statement may be described as analytic simply when it is synonymous with a logically true statement.

So, if the verification theory can be accepted as an adequate account of statement synonymy, the notion of analyticity is saved after all. However, let us reflect. Statement synonymy is said to be likeness of method of empirical confirmation or infirmation. Just what are these methods which are to be compared for

6. The doctrine can indeed be formulated with terms rather than statements as the units. Thus C. I. Lewis describes the meaning of a term as "*a criterion in mind,* by reference to which one is able to apply or refuse to apply the expression in question in the case of presented, or imagined, things or situations" (Carnap, *Meaning and Necessity,* p. 133).

likeness? What, in other words, is the nature of the relationship between a statement and the experiences which contribute to or detract from its confirmation?

The most naive view of the relationship is that it is one of direct report. This is *radical reductionism*. Every meaningful statement is held to be translatable into a statement (true or false) about immediate experience. Radical reductionism, in one form or another, well antedates the verification theory of meaning explicitly so called. Thus Locke and Hume held that every idea must either originate directly in sense experience or else be compounded of ideas thus originating; and taking a hint from Tooke [7] we might rephrase this doctrine in semantical jargon by saying that a term, to be significant at all, must be either a name of a sense datum or a compound of such names or an abbreviation of such a compound. So stated, the doctrine remains ambiguous as between sense data as sensory events and sense data as sensory qualities; and it remains vague as to the admissible ways of compounding. Moreover, the doctrine is unnecessarily and intolerably restrictive in the term-by-term critique which it imposes. More reasonably, and without yet exceeding the limits of what I have called radical reductionism, we may take full statements as our significant units—thus demanding that our statements as wholes be translatable into sense-datum language, but not that they be translatable term by term.

This emendation would unquestionably have been welcome to Locke and Hume and Tooke, but historically it had to await two intermediate developments. One of these developments was the increasing emphasis on verification or confirmation, which came with the explicitly so-called verification theory of meaning. The objects of verification or confirmation being statements, this emphasis gave the statement an ascendency over the word or term as unit of significant discourse. The other development, consequent upon the first, was Russell's discovery of the concept of incomplete symbols defined in use.

Radical reductionism, conceived now with statements as units, sets itself the task of specifying a sense-datum language and

7. John Horne Tooke, *The Diversions of Purley* (London, 1776; Boston, 1806), I, ch. ii.

showing how to translate the rest of significant discourse, statement by statement, into it. Carnap embarked on this project in
the *Aufbau*.[8]

  The language which Carnap adopted as his starting point was
not a sense-datum language in the narrowest conceivable sense,
for it included also the notations of logic, up through higher set
theory. In effect it included the whole language of pure mathematics. The ontology implicit in it (i.e., the range of values of
its variables) embraced not only sensory events but classes,
classes of classes, and so on. Empiricists there are who would
boggle at such prodigality. Carnap's starting point is very par-
simonious, however, in its extralogical or sensory part. In a series
of constructions in which he exploits the resources of modern
logic with much ingenuity, he succeeds in defining a wide array
of important additional sensory concepts which, but for his
constructions, one would not have dreamed were definable on
so slender a basis. Carnap was the first empiricist who, not content with asserting the reducibility of science to terms of immediate experience, took serious steps toward carrying out the
reduction.

  Even supposing Carnap's starting point satisfactory, his constructions were, as he himself stressed, only a fragment of the
full program. The construction of even the simplest statements
about the physical world was left in a sketchy state. Carnap's
suggestions on this subject were, despite their sketchiness, very
suggestive. He explained spatio-temporal point-instants as quad-
ruples of real numbers and envisaged assignment of sense
qualities to point-instants according to certain canons. Roughly
summarized, the plan was that qualities should be assigned to
point-instants in such a way as to achieve the laziest world compatible with our experience. The principle of least action was to
be our guide in consructing a world from experience.

  Carnap did not seem to recognize, however, that his treatment of physical objects fell short of reduction not merely
through sketchiness, but in principle. Statements of the form
'Quality $q$ is at point-instant $x;$ $y;$ $z;$ $t$' were, according to his
canons, to be apportioned truth values in such a way as to

8. R. Carnap, *Der logische Aufbau der Welt* (Berlin, 1928).

maximize and minimize certain over-all features, and with growth of experience the truth values were to be progressively revised in the same spirit. I think this is a good schematization (deliberately oversimplified, to be sure) of what science really does; but it provides no indication, not even the sketchiest, of how a statement of the form 'Quality $q$ is at $x; y; z; t$' could ever be translated into Carnap's initial language of sense data and logic. The connective 'is at' remains an added undefined connective; the canons counsel us in its use but not in its elimination.

Carnap seems to have appreciated this point afterward; for in his later writings he abandoned all notion of the translatability of statements about the physical world into statements about immediate experience. Reductionism in its radical form has long since ceased to figure in Carnap's philosophy.

But the dogma of reductionism has, in a subtler and more tenuous form, continued to influence the thought of empiricists. The notion lingers that to each statement, or each synthetic statement, there is associated a unique range of possible sensory events such that the occurrence of any of them would add to the likelihood of truth of the statement, and that there is associated also another unique range of possible sensory events whose occurrence would detract from that likelihood. This notion is of course implicit in the verification theory of meaning.

The dogma of reductionism survives in the supposition that each statement, taken in isolation from its fellows, can admit of confirmation or infirmation at all. My countersuggestion, issuing essentially from Carnap's doctrine of the physical world in the *Aufbau,* is that our statements about the external world face the tribunal of sense experience not individually but only as a corporate body.

The dogma of reductionism, even in its attenuated form, is intimately connected with the other dogma: that there is a cleavage between the analytic and the synthetic. We have found ourselves led, indeed, from the latter problem to the former through the verification theory of meaning. More directly, the one dogma clearly supports the other in this way: as long as it is taken to be significant in general to speak of the con-

firmation and infirmation of a statement, it seems significant to
speak also of a limiting kind of statement which is vacuously
confirmed, *ipso facto*, come what may; and such a statement is
analytic.

The two dogmas are, indeed, at root identical. We lately
reflected that in general the truth of statements does obviously
depend both upon language and upon extra-linguistic fact; and
we noted that this obvious circumstance carries in its train, not
logically but all too naturally, a feeling that the truth of a
statement is somehow analyzable into a linguistic component
and a factual component. The factual component must, if we are
empiricists, boil down to a range of confirmatory experiences.
In the extreme case where the linguistic component is all that
matters, a true statement is analytic. But I hope we are now
impressed with how stubbornly the distinction between analytic
and synthetic has resisted any straightforward drawing. I am
impressed also, apart from prefabricated examples of black and
white balls in an urn, with how baffling the problem has always
been of arriving at any explicit theory of the empirical confirmation of a synthetic statement. My present suggestion is that it is
nonsense, and the root of much nonsense, to speak of a linguistic component and a factual component in the truth of any
individual statement. Taken collectively, science has its double
dependence upon language and experience; but this duality is
not significantly traceable into the statements of science taken
one by one.

Russell's concept of definition in use was, as remarked, an
advance over the impossible term-by-term empiricism of Locke
and Hume. The statement, rather than the term, came with
Russell to be recognized as the unit accountable to an empiricist
critique. But what I am now urging is that even in taking the
statement as unit we have drawn our grid too finely. The unit
of empirical significance is the whole of science.

### VI. EMPIRICISM WITHOUT THE DOGMAS

The totality of our so-called knowledge or beliefs, from the most
casual matters of geography and history to the profoundest laws

of atomic physics or even of pure mathematics and logic, is a man-made fabric which impinges on experience only along the edges. Or, to change the figure, total science is like a field of force whose boundary conditions are experience. A conflict with experience at the periphery occasions readjustments in the interior of the field. Truth values have to be redistributed over some of our statements. Re-evaluation of some statements entails re-evaluation of others, because of their logical interconnections —the logical laws being in turn simply certain further statements of the system, certain further elements of the field. Having re-evaluated one statement we must re-evaluate some others, whether they be statements logically connected with the first or whether they be the statements of logical connections themselves. But the total field is so undetermined by its boundary conditions, experience, that there is much latitude of choice as to what statements to re-evaluate in the light of any single contrary experience. No particular experiences are linked with any particular statements in the interior of the field, except indirectly through considerations of equilibrium affecting the field as a whole.

If this view is right, it is misleading to speak of the empirical content of an individual statement—especially if it be a statement at all remote from the experiential periphery of the field. Furthermore it becomes folly to seek a boundary between synthetic statements, which hold contingently on experience, and analytic statements which hold come what may. Any statement can be held true come what may, if we make drastic enough adjustments elsewhere in the system. Even a statement very close to the periphery can be held true in the face of recalcitrant experience by pleading hallucination or by amending certain statements of the kind called logical laws. Conversely, by the same token, no statement is immune to revision. Revision even of the logical law of the excluded middle has been proposed as a means of simplifying quantum mechanics; and what difference is there in principle between such a shift and the shift whereby Kepler superseded Ptolemy, or Einstein Newton, or Darwin Aristotle?

For vividness I have been speaking in terms of varying dis-

tances from a sensory periphery. Let me try now to clarify this
notion without metaphor. Certain statements, though *about*
physical objects and not sense experience, seem peculiarly germane to sense experience—and in a selective way: some statements to some experiences, others to others. Such statements, especially germane to particular experiences, I picture as
near the periphery. But in this relation of "germaneness" I
envisage nothing more than a loose association reflecting the
relative likelihood, in practice, of our choosing one statement
rather than another for revision in the event of recalcitrant
experience. For example, we can imagine recalcitrant experiences
to which we would surely be inclined to accommodate our
system by re-evaluating just the statement that there are brick
houses on Elm Street, together with related statements on the
same topic. We can imagine other recalcitrant experiences to
which we would be inclined to accommodate our system by
re-evaluating just the statement that there are no centaurs, along
with kindred statements. A recalcitrant experience can, I have
already urged, be accommodated by any of various alternative
re-evaluations in various alternative quarters of the total system;
but, in the cases which we are now imagining, our natural
tendency to disturb the total system as little as possible would
lead us to focus our revisions upon these specific statements
concerning brick houses or centaurs. These statements are felt,
therefore, to have a sharper empirical reference than highly
theoretical statements of physics or logic or ontology. The latter
statements may be thought of as relatively centrally located
within the total network, meaning merely that little preferential
connection with any particular sense data obtrudes itself.

As an empiricist I continue to think of the conceptual scheme
of science as a tool, ultimately, for predicting future experience
in the light of past experience. Physical objects are conceptually
imported into the situation as convenient intermediaries—not by
definition in terms of experience, but simply as irreducible posits
comparable, epistemologically, to the gods of Homer. Let me
interject that for my part I do, qua lay physicist, believe in
physical objects and not in Homer's gods; and I consider it a
scientific error to believe otherwise. But in point of epistemo-

logical footing the physical objects and the gods differ only in degree and not in kind. Both sorts of entities enter our conception only as cultural posits. The myth of physical objects is epistemologically superior to most in that it has proved more efficacious than other myths as a device for working a manageable structure into the flux of experience.

Imagine, for the sake of analogy, that we are given the rational numbers. We develop an algebraic theory for reasoning about them, but we find it inconveniently complex, because certain functions such as square root lack values for some arguments. Then it is discovered that the rules of our algebra can be much simplified by conceptually augmenting our ontology with some mythical entities, to be called irrational numbers. All we continue to be really interested in, first and last, are rational numbers; but we find that we can commonly get from one law about rational numbers to another much more quickly and simply by pretending that the irrational numbers are there too.

I think this a fair account of the introduction of irrational numbers and other extensions of the number system. The fact that the mythical status of irrational numbers eventually gave way to the Dedekind-Russell version of them as certain infinite classes of ratios is irrelevant to my analogy. That version is impossible anyway as long as reality is limited to the rational numbers and not extended to classes of them.

Now I suggest that experience is analogous to the rational numbers and that the physical objects, in analogy to the irrational numbers, are posits which serve merely to simplify our treatment of experience. The physical objects are no more reducible to experience than the irrational numbers to rational numbers, but their incorporation into the theory enables us to get more easily from one statement about experience to another.

The salient differences between the positing of physical objects and the positing of irrational numbers are, I think, just two. First, the factor of simplication is more overwhelming in the case of physical objects than in the numerical case. Second, the positing of physical objects is far more archaic, being indeed coeval, I expect, with language itself. For language is social and so depends for its development upon intersubjective reference.

Positing does not stop with macroscopic physical objects. Objects at the atomic level and beyond are posited to make the laws of macroscopic objects, and ultimately the laws of experience, simpler and more manageable; and we need not expect or demand full definition of atomic and subatomic entities in terms of macroscopic ones, any more than definition of macroscopic things in terms of sense data. Science is a continuation of common sense, and it continues the common-sense expedient of swelling ontology to simplify theory.

Physical objects, small and large, are not the only posits. Forces are another example; and indeed we are told nowadays that the boundary between energy and matter is obsolete. Moreover, the abstract entities which are the substance of mathematics—ultimately classes and classes of classes and so on up—are another posit in the same spirit. Epistemologically these are myths on the same footing with physical objects and gods, neither better nor worse except for differences in the degree to which they expedite our dealings with sense experiences.

The over-all algebra of rational and irrational numbers is underdetermined by the algebra of rational numbers, but is smoother and more convenient; and it includes the algebra of rational numbers as a jagged or gerrymandered part. Total science, mathematical and natural and human, is similarly but more extremely underdetermined by experience. The edge of the system must be kept squared with experience; the rest, with all its elaborate myths or fictions, has as its objective the simplicity of laws.

Ontological questions, under this view, are on a par with questions of natural science. Consider the question whether to countenance classes as entities. This, as I have argued elsewhere,[9] is the question whether to quantify with respect to variables which take classes as values. Now Carnap has maintained [10] that this is a question not of matters of fact but of choosing a convenient language form, a convenient conceptual

9. For example, in "Notes on Existence and Necessity," *Journal of Philosophy*, 11 (1943), 113–127.

10. Carnap, "Empiricism, Semantics, and Ontology," *Revue internationale de philosophie*, 4 (1950), 20–40.

scheme or framework for science. With this I agree, but only on the proviso that the same be conceded regarding scientific hypotheses generally. Carnap has recognized [11] that he is able to preserve a double standard for ontological questions and scientific hypotheses only by assuming an absolute distinction between the analytic and the synthetic; and I need not say again that this is a distinction which I reject.

Some issues do, I grant, seem more a question of convenient conceptual scheme and others more a question of brute fact. The issue over there being classes seems more a question of convenient conceptual scheme; the issue over there being centaurs, or brick houses on Elm Street, seems more a question of fact. But I have been urging that this difference is only one of degree, and that it turns upon our vaguely pragmatic inclination to adjust one strand of the fabric of science rather than another in accommodating some particular recalcitrant experience. Conservatism figures in such choices, and so does the quest for simplicity.

Carnap, Lewis, and others take a pragmatic stand on the question of choosing between language forms, scientific frameworks; but their pragmatism leaves off at the imagined boundary between the analytic and the synthetic. In repudiating such a boundary I espouse a more thorough pragmatism. Each man is given a scientific heritage plus a continuing barrage of sensory stimulation; and the considerations which guide him in warping his scientific heritage to fit his continuing sensory promptings are, where rational, pragmatic.

---

11. Carnap, "Empiricism, Semantics, and Ontology," p. 32.

# IN DEFENSE OF A DOGMA

## H. P. Grice

## and P. F. Strawson

*Grice and Strawson argue, in "In Defense of a Dogma," that there is a distinction between analytic and synthetic statements, and that Quine's conditions for adequately drawing the distinction are too stringent. They argue that since the terms 'analytic' and 'synthetic' have an established use with respect to an open list of statements, they do mark a distinction.*

*Further, they assert that this is not merely a matter of philosopher's terminology: for Quine's argument rests, in part, upon the possibility of distinguishing between having the same meaning and not having the same meaning, which is not a philosopher's notion. Retreat to professional sanctuary is not a possible resort for Quine. If the notion of having the same meaning is meaningless, then so is the notion of having a meaning at all— a possible* reductio *on Quine's argument.*

From *The Philosophical Review*, vol. 65, 1956. Reprinted by permission of *The Philosophical Review* and the authors.

*Quine's strictures are unreasonable, because he requires a strict definition of one of a set of interdefinable terms without using any other member of the set, when there are less formal, but perfectly adequate ways of explaining the import of expressions belonging to the set: consider their isolation of logical possibility.*

*Moreover, Quine's position is incoherent, because he understands synonymy by stipulation, but claims not to understand other forms of synonymy. Grice and Strawson further argue that there are cases (one of Quine's own paragraphs, for example) where we would hesitate over ascribing 'true' just as much as we would hesitate over ascribing 'analytic.' And just as this does not imply that 'true' is hopelessly obscure, likewise, Quine's arguments do not show that 'analytic' is hopelessly obscure.*

*The remainder of "In Defense of a Dogma" is devoted to showing that Quine's constructive theory does not necessitate rejecting the distinction between analytic statements and synthetic statements. There is not space enough to give these arguments the consideration they deserve. But since our concern is with the distinction itself, it is not necessary to do more than to commend them to the reader.*

*Following are some of the reflections prompted by "In Defense of a Dogma." Does Quine literally and explicitly deny that there is a distinction between analytic statements and synthetic statements? Could not he maintain that the distinction be arbitrarily drawn relative to the amount of unwillingness generally to sacrifice a given statement? And will the sample explanation of logical possibility serve as an example of explaining the distinction, since Quine has already exempted logical truths (and, presumably, logical falsehoods) from his attack? Moreover, does Quine in fact take the step from "We have not made satisfactory sense (provided a satisfactory explanation) of x" to "x does not make sense?" Could not Quine reply to the charge of incoherence with the rejoinder that stipulated synonymy, synonymy by fiat, and other sorts of synonymy are entirely different beasts, and that having tamed the one, it is not always possible to know how to tame the other? To the charge that his demands are unreasonable, could not Quine take the White gambit, and ask merely for some clarification, clarification not yielded by the example of 'logically possible,' the latter presumably already having been exempted? Lastly, other writings of Quine suggest that he would not be at all averse to giving up the notion of "having a meaning" (though not that of being meaningful), thus pulling the sting of the reductio.*

In his article "Two Dogmas of Empiricism," [1] Professor Quine advances a number of criticisms of the supposed distinction between analytic and synthetic statements, and of other associated notions. It is, he says, a distinction which he rejects.[2] We wish to show that his criticisms of the distinction do not justify his rejection of it.

There are many ways in which a distinction can be criticized, and more than one in which it can be rejected. It can be criticized for not being a sharp distinction (for admitting of cases which do not fall clearly on either side of it); or on the ground that the terms in which it is customarily drawn are ambiguous (have more than one meaning); or on the ground that it is confused (the different meanings being habitually conflated). Such criticisms alone would scarcely amount to a rejection of the distinction. They would, rather, be a prelude to clarification. It is not this sort of criticism which Quine makes.

Again, a distinction can be criticized on the ground that it is not useful. It can be said to be useless for certain purposes, or useless altogether, and, perhaps, pedantic. One who criticizes in this way may indeed be said to reject a distinction, but in a sense which also requires him to acknowledge its existence. He simply declares he can get on without it. But Quine's rejection of the analytic-synthetic distinction appears to be more radical than this. He would certainly say he could get on without the distinction, but not in a sense which would commit him to acknowledging its existence.

Or again, one could criticize the way or ways in which a distinction is customarily expounded or explained on the ground

---

1. W. V. O. Quine, *From a Logical Point of View* (Cambridge, Mass., 1953), pp. 20–46. All references are to page numbers in this book.
2. Page 46.

that these explanations did not make it really clear. And Quine certainly makes such criticisms in the case of the analytic-synthetic distinction.

But he does, or seems to do, a great deal more. He declares, or seems to declare, not merely that the distinction is useless or inadequately clarified, but also that it is altogether illusory, that the belief in its existence is a philosophical mistake. "That there is such a distinction to be drawn at all," he says, "is an unempirical dogma of empiricists, a metaphysical article of faith." [3] It is the existence of the distinction that he here calls in question; so his rejection of it would seem to amount to a denial of its existence.

Evidently such a position of extreme skepticism about a distinction is not in general justified merely by criticisms, however just in themselves, of philosophical attempts to clarify it. There are doubtless plenty of distinctions, drawn in philosophy and outside it, which still await adequate philosophical elucidation, but which few would want on this account to declare illusory. Quine's article, however, does not consist wholly, though it does consist largely, in criticizing attempts at elucidation. He does try also to diagnose the causes of the belief in the distinction, and he offers some positive doctrine, acceptance of which he represents as incompatible with this belief. If there is any general prior presumption in favor of the existence of the distinction, it seems that Quine's radical rejection of it must rest quite heavily on this part of his article, since the force of any such presumption is not even impaired by philosophical failures to clarify a distinction so supported.

Is there such a presumption in favor of the distinction's existence? Prima facie, it must be admitted that there is. An appeal to philosophical tradition is perhaps unimpressive and is certainly unnecessary. But it is worth pointing out that Quine's objection is not simply to the words "analytic" and "synthetic," but to a distinction which they are supposed to express, and which at different times philosophers have supposed themselves to be expressing by means of such pairs of words or phrases as "necessary" and "contingent," "a priori" and "empirical," "truth of

3. Page 37.

reason" and "truth of fact"; so Quine is certainly at odds with a philosophical tradition which is long and not wholly disreputable. But there is no need to appeal only to tradition; for there is also present practice. We can appeal, that is, to the fact that those who use the terms "analytic" and "synthetic" do to a very considerable extent agree in the applications they make of them. They apply the term "analytic" to more or less the same cases, withhold it from more or less the same cases, and hesitate over more or less the same cases. This agreement extends not only to cases which they have been *taught* so to characterize, but to new cases. In short, "analytic" and "synthetic" have a more or less established philosophical *use;* and this seems to suggest that it is absurd, even senseless, to say that there is no such distinction. For, in general, if a pair of contrasting expressions are habitually and generally used in application to the same cases, *where these cases do not form a closed list,* this is a sufficient condition for saying that there are *kinds* of cases to which the expressions apply; and nothing more is needed for them to mark a distinction.

In view of the possibility of this kind of argument, one may begin to doubt whether Quine really holds the extreme thesis which his words encourage one to attribute to him. It is for this reason that we made the attribution tentative. For on at least one natural interpretation of this extreme thesis, when we say of something true that it is analytic and of another true thing that it is synthetic, it simply never is the case that we thereby mark a distinction between them. And this view seems terribly difficult to reconcile with the fact of an established philosophical usage (i.e., of general agreement in application in an open class). For this reason, Quine's thesis might be better represented not as the thesis that there is *no difference at all* marked by the use of these expressions, but as the thesis that the nature of, and reasons for, the difference or differences are totally misunderstood by those who use the expressions, that the stories they tell themselves *about* the difference are full of illusion.

We think Quine might be prepared to accept this amendment. If so, it could, in the following way, be made the basis of something like an answer to the argument which prompted it. Philosophers are notoriously subject to illusion, and to mistaken theories. Suppose there were a particular mistaken theory about language or knowledge, such that, seen in the light of this theory, some statements (or propositions or sentences) appeared to have a characteristic which no statements really have, or even, perhaps, which it does not make sense to suppose that any statement has, and which no one who was not consciously or subconsciously influenced by this theory would ascribe to any statement. And suppose that there were other statements which, seen in this light, did not appear to have this characteristic, and others again which presented an uncertain appearance. Then philosophers who were under the influence of this theory would tend to mark the supposed presence or absence of this characteristic by a pair of contrasting expressions, say "analytic" and "synthetic." Now in these circumstances it still could not be said that there was no distinction at all being marked by the use of these expressions, for there would be at least the distinction we have just described (the distinction, namely, between those statements which appeared to have and those which appeared to lack a certain characteristic), and there might well be other assignable differences too, which would account for the difference in appearance; but it certainly could be said that *the* difference these philosophers supposed themselves to be marking by the use of the expressions simply did not exist, and perhaps also (supposing the characteristic in question to be one which it was absurd to ascribe to any statement) that these expressions, as so used, were senseless or without meaning. We should only have to suppose that such a mistaken theory was very plausible and attractive, in order to reconcile the fact of an established philosophical usage for a pair of contrasting terms with the claim that *the* distinction which the terms purported to mark did not exist at all, though not with the claim that there simply did not exist a difference of any kind between the classes of statements so characterized. We think that the former claim would probably be sufficient for Quine's purposes. But to establish such a claim on the sort of grounds we have indicated evidently requires a great deal more argument than is involved in showing that certain explanations of a term do not measure up to certain requirements of adequacy in philosophical clarification—and not only more argument, but argument of a very different kind. For it would surely be too harsh to maintain that the *general* presumption is that philosophical distinctions embody the kind of illusion we have described. On the whole, it seems that philosophers are prone to make too few distinctions rather than too many. It is their assimilations, rather than their distinctions, which tend to be spurious.

So far we have argued as if the prior presumption in favor of the existence of the distinction which Quine questions rested solely on the fact of an agreed *philosophical* usage for the terms "analytic" and "synthetic." A presumption with only this basis could no doubt be countered by a strategy such as we have just outlined. But, in fact, if we are to accept Quine's account of the matter, the presumption in question is not only so based. For among the notions which belong to the analyticity-group is one which Quine calls "cognitive synonymy," and in terms of which he allows that the notion of analyticity could at any rate be formally explained. Unfortunately, he adds, the notion of cognitive synonymy is just as unclarified as that of analyticity. To say that two expressions $x$ and $y$ are cognitively synonymous seems to correspond, at any rate roughly, to what we should ordinarily express by saying that $x$ and $y$ have the same meaning or that $x$ means the same as $y$. If Quine is to be consistent in his adherence to the extreme thesis, then it appears that he must maintain not only that the distinction we suppose ourselves to be marking by the use of the terms "analytic" and "synthetic" does not exist, but also that the distinction we suppose ourselves to be marking by the use of the expressions "means the same as," "does not mean the same as" does not exist either. At least, he must maintain this insofar as the notion of *meaning the same as,* in its application to predicate-expressions, is supposed to differ from and go beyond the notion of *being true of just the same objects as.* (This latter notion—which we might call that of "coextensionality"—he is prepared to allow to be intelligible, though, as he rightly says, it is not sufficient for the explanation of analyticity.) Now since he cannot claim this time that the pair of expressions in question (viz., "means the same," "does not mean the same") is the special property of philosophers, the strategy outlined above of countering the presumption in favor of their marking a genuine distinction is not available here (or is at least enormously less plausible). Yet the denial that the distinction (taken as different from the distinction between the coextensional and the non-coextensional) really exists, is extremely paradoxical. It involves saying, for example, that anyone who seriously remarks that "bachelor" means the same as "unmarried man" but that "creature with kidneys" does not mean the same as "creature with a heart"—supposing the last two expressions to be coextensional—*either* is not in fact drawing attention to any distinction at all between the relations between the members of each pair of expressions *or* is making a philosophical mistake about the nature of the distinction between them. In either case, what he says, taken as he intends it to be taken, is senseless or absurd. More generally, it involves saying that it is always senseless or absurd to make a statement of the form "Predicates $x$ and $y$ in fact apply to the same objects, but do not have the same meaning." But the paradox is more violent than this. For we frequently talk of the presence or absence of relations of synonymy between kinds of expressions—for example, conjunctions, particles of many kinds, whole sentences— where there does not appear to be any obvious substitute for the ordinary notion of synonymy, in the way in which coextensionality is said to be a substitute for synonymy of predicates. Is all such talk meaningless? Is all talk of correct or incorrect *translation* of sentences of one language into sentences of another meaningless? It is hard to believe that it is. But if we do successfully make the effort to believe it, we have still harder renunciations before us. If talk of sentence-synonymy is meaningless, then it seems that talk of sentences having a meaning at all must be meaningless too. For if it made sense to talk of a sentence having a meaning, or meaning something, then presumably it would make sense to ask "What does it mean?" And if it made sense to ask "What does it mean?" of a sentence, then sentence-synonymy could be roughly defined as follows: Two sentences are synonymous if and only if any true answer to the question "What does it mean?" asked of one of them, is a true

answer to the same question, asked of the other. We do not, of
course, claim any clarifying power for this definition. We want
only to point out that if we are to give up the notion of sentence-
synonymy as senseless, we must give up the notion of sentence-
significance (of a sentence having meaning) as senseless too.
But then perhaps we might as well give up the notion of sense—
It seems clear that we have here a typical example of a philosopher's paradox. Instead of examining the actual use that we make
of the notion of *meaning the same*, the philosopher measures it
by some perhaps inappropriate standard (in this case some
standard of clarifiability), and because it falls short of this standard, or seems to do so, denies its reality, declares it illusory.

We have argued so far that there is a strong presumption in
favor of the existence of the distinction, or distinctions, which
Quine challenges—a presumption resting both on philosophical
and on ordinary usage—and that this presumption is not in the
least shaken by the fact, if it is a fact, that the distinctions in
question have not been, in some sense, adequately clarified.
It is perhaps time to look at what Quine's notion of adequate
clarification is.

The main theme of his article can be roughly summarized as
follows. There is a certain circle or family of expressions, of
which "analytic" is one, such that if any one member of the
circle could be taken to be satisfactorily understood or explained,
then other members of the circle could be verbally, and hence
satisfactorily, explained in terms of it. Other members of the
family are: "self-contradictory" (in a broad sense), "necessary,"
"synonymous," "semantical rule," and perhaps (but again in a
broad sense) "definition." The list could be added to. Unfortunately each member of the family is in as great need of
explanation as any other. We give some sample quotations: "The
notion of self-contradictoriness (in the required broad sense of
inconsistency) stands in exactly the same need of clarification
as does the notion of analyticity itself." [4] Again, Quine speaks of
"a notion of synonymy which is in no less need of clarification
than analyticity itself." [5] Again, of the adverb "necessarily," as a

4. Page 20.
5. Page 23.

candidate for use in the explanation of synonymy, he says, "Does the adverb *really make sense?* To suppose that it does is to suppose that we have already *made satisfactory sense* of 'analytic.'" [6] To make "satisfactory sense" of one of these expressions would seem to involve two things. (1) It would seem to involve providing an explanation which does not incorporate any expression belonging to the family-circle. (2) It would seem that the explanation provided must be of the same general character as those rejected explanations which do incorporate members of the family-circle (i.e., it must specify some feature common and peculiar to all cases to which, for example the, word "analytic" is to be applied; it must have the same general form as an explanation beginning, "a statement is analytic if and only if . . ."). It is true that Quine does not explicitly state the second requirement; but since he does not even consider the question whether any other kind of explanation would be relevant, it seems reasonable to attribute it to him. If we take these two conditions together, and generalize the result, it would seem that Quine requires of a satisfactory explanation of an expression that it should take the form of a pretty strict definition but should not make use of any member of a group of interdefinable terms to which the expression belongs. We may well begin to feel that a satisfactory explanation is hard to come by. The other element in Quine's position is one we have already commented on in general, before enquiring what (according to him) is to count as a satisfactory explanation. It is the step from "We have not made satisfactory sense (provided a satisfactory explanation) of *x*" to "*x* does not make sense."

It would seem fairly clearly unreasonable to insist *in general* that the availability of a satisfactory explanation in the sense sketched above is a necessary condition of an expression's making sense. It is perhaps dubious whether *any* such explanations can *ever* be given. (The hope that they can be is, or was, the hope of reductive analysis in general.) Even if such explanations can be given in some cases, it would be pretty generally agreed that there are other cases in which they cannot. One might think, for example, of the group of expressions which

6. Page 30, our italics.

includes "morally wrong," "blameworthy," "breach of moral rules," etc.; or of the group which includes the propositional connectives and the words "true" and "false," "statement," "fact," "denial," "assertion." Few people would want to say that the expressions belonging to either of these groups were senseless on the ground that they have not been formally defined (or even on the ground that it was impossible formally to define them) except in terms of members of the same group. It might, however, be said that while the unavailability of a satisfactory explanation in the special sense described was not a *generally* sufficient reason for declaring that a given expression was senseless, it was a sufficient reason in the case of the expressions of the analyticity-group. But anyone who said this would have to advance a reason for discriminating in this way against the expressions of this group. The only plausible reason for being harder on these expressions than on others is a refinement on a consideration which we have already had before us. It starts from the point that "analytic" and "synthetic" themselves are technical philosophical expressions. To the rejoinder that other expressions of the family concerned, such as "means the same as," or "is inconsistent with," or "self-contradictory," are not at all technical expressions, but are common property, the reply would doubtless be that, to qualify for inclusion in the family circle, these expressions have to be used in specially adjusted and precise senses (or pseudo-senses) which they do not ordinarily possess. It is the fact, then, that all the terms belonging to the circle are *either* technical terms *or* ordinary terms used in specially adjusted senses, that might be held to justify us in being particularly suspicious of the claims of members of the circle to have any sense at all, and hence to justify us in requiring them to pass a test for significance which would admittedly be too stringent if generally applied. This point has some force, though we doubt if the special adjustments spoken of are in every case as considerable as it suggests. (This seems particularly doubtful in the case of the word "inconsistent"—a perfectly good member of the nontechnician's meta-logical vocabulary.) But though the point has some force, it does not have whatever force would be required to justify us in insisting that the expressions concerned should pass exactly that test for significance which is in question. The fact, if it is a fact, that the expressions cannot be explained in precisely the way which Quine seems to require, does not mean that they cannot be explained at all. There is no need to try to pass them off as expressing innate ideas. They can be and are explained, though in other and less formal ways than that which Quine considers. (And the fact that they are so explained fits with the facts, first, that there is a generally agreed philosophical use for them, and second, that this use is technical or specially adjusted.) To illustrate the point briefly for one member of the analyticity family. Let us suppose we are trying to explain to someone the notion of *logical impossibility* (a member of the family which Quine presumably regards as no clearer than any of the others) and we decide to do it by bringing out the contrast between logical and natural (or causal) impossibility. We might take as our examples the logical impossibility of a child of three's being an adult, and the natural impossibility of a child of three's understanding Russell's Theory of Types. We might instruct our pupil to imagine two conversations one of which begins by someone (X) making the claim:

(1) "My neighbor's three-year-old child understands Russell's Theory of Types,"

and the other of which begins by someone (Y) making the claim:

(1') "My neighbor's three-year-old child is an adult."

It would not be inappropriate to reply to X, taking the remark as a hyperbole:

(2) "You mean the child is a particularly bright lad."

If X were to say:

(3) "No, I mean what I say—he really does understand it,"

one might be inclined to reply:

(4) "I don't believe you—the thing's impossible."

But if the child were then produced, and did (as one knows he would not) expound the theory correctly, answer questions on it, criticize it, and so on, one would in the end be forced to acknowledge that the claim was literally true and that the child was a prodigy. Now consider one's reaction to Y's claim. To begin with, it might be somewhat similar to the previous case. One might say:

(2′) "You mean he's uncommonly sensible or very advanced for his age."

If Y replies:

(3′) "No, I mean what I say,"

we might reply:

(4′) "Perhaps you mean that he won't grow any more, or that he's a sort of freak, that he's already fully developed."

Y replies:

(5′) "No, he's not a freak, he's just an adult."

At this stage—or possibly if we are patient, a little later—we shall be inclined to say that we just don't understand what Y is saying, and to suspect that he just does not know the meaning of some of the words he is using. For unless he is prepared to admit that he is using words in a figurative or unusual sense, we shall say, not that we don't believe him, but that his words have *no* sense. And whatever kind of creature is ultimately produced for our inspection, it will not lead us to say that what Y said was literally true, but at most to say that we now see what he meant. As a summary of the difference between the two imaginary conversations, we might say that in both cases we would tend to begin by supposing that the other speaker was using words in a figurative or unusual or restricted way; but in the face of his repeated claim to be speaking literally, it would be appropriate in the first case to say that we did not believe him and in the second case to say that we did not understand him. If, like Pascal, we thought it prudent to prepare against very long chances, we should in the first case know what to prepare for; in the second, we should have no idea.

We give this as an example of just one type of informal explanation which we might have recourse to in the case of one notion of the analyticity group. (We do not wish to suggest it is the only type.) Further examples, with different though connected types of treatment, might be necessary to teach our pupil the use of the notion of logical impossibility in its application to

more complicated cases—if indeed he did not pick it up from
the one case. Now of course this type of explanation does not
yield a formal statement of necessary and sufficient conditions
for the application of the notion concerned. So it does not fulfill
one of the conditions which Quine seems to require of a satisfactory explanation. On the other hand, it does appear to fulfill the
other. It breaks out of the family-circle. The distinction in which
we ultimately come to rest is that between not believing something and not understanding something; or between incredulity
yielding to conviction, and incomprehension yielding to comprehension. It would be rash to maintain that *this* distinction does
not need clarification; but it would be absurd to maintain that
it does not exist. In the face of the availability of this informal
type of explanation for the notions of the analyticity group, the
fact that they have not received another type of explanation
(which it is dubious whether *any* expressions *ever* receive)
seems a wholly inadequate ground for the conclusion that the
notions are pseudo-notions, that the expressions which purport
to express them have no sense. To say this is not to deny that it
would be philosophically desirable, and a proper object of philosophical endeavor, to find a more illuminating general characterization of the notions of this group than any that has been so
far given. But the question of how, if at all, this can be done is
quite irrelevant to the question of whether or not the expressions
which belong to the circle have an intelligible use and mark
genuine distinctions.

So far we have tried to show that sections 1 to 4 of Quine's
article—the burden of which is that the notions of the analyticity
group have not been satisfactorily explained—do not establish
the extreme thesis for which he appears to be arguing. It remains
to be seen whether sections 5 and 6, in which diagnosis and positive theory are offered, are any more sucessful. But before we
turn to them, there are two further points worth making which
arise out of the first two sections.

(1) One concerns what Quine says about *definition* and *synonymy*. He remarks that definition does not, as some have supposed, "hold the key to synonymy and analyticity," since "definition—except in the extreme case of the explicitly conventional

introduction of new notations—hinges on prior relations of synonymy." [7] But now consider what he says of these extreme cases.
He says: "Here the definiendum becomes synonymous with the
definiens simply because it has been expressly created for the
purpose of being synonymous with the definiens. Here we have
a really transparent case of synonymy created by definition;
would that all species of synonymy were as intelligible." Now if
we are to take these words of Quine seriously, then his position
*as a whole* is incoherent. It is like the position of a man to whom
we are trying to explain, say, the idea of one thing fitting into another thing, or two things fitting together, and who says: "I can
understand what it means to say that one thing fits into another,
or that two things fit together, in the case where one was specially made to fit the other, but I cannot understand what it
means to say this in any other case." Perhaps we should not take
Quine's words here too seriously. But if not, then we have the
right to ask him exactly what state of affairs he thinks *is* brought
about by explicit definition, what relation between expressions *is*
established by this procedure, and why he thinks it unintelligible
to suggest that the same (or a closely analogous) state of affairs,
or relation, should exist in the absence of this procedure. For our
part, we should be inclined to take Quine's words (or some of
them) seriously, and reverse his conclusions; and maintain that
the notion of synonymy by explicit convention would be unintelligible if the notion of synonymy by usage were not presupposed. There cannot be law where there is no custom, or
rules where there are not practices (though perhaps we can
understand better what a practice is by looking at a rule).

(2) The second point arises out of a paragraph on page 32 of
Quine's book. We quote:

> I do not know whether the statement "Everything green is
> extended" is analytic. Now does my indecision over this ex-
> ample really betray an incomplete understanding, an incom-
> plete grasp, of the "meanings" of "green" and "extended"? I
> think not. The trouble is not with "green" or "extended," but
> with "analytic."

7. Page 27.

If, as Quine says, the trouble is with "analytic," then the trouble should doubtless disappear when "analytic" is removed. So let us remove it, and replace it with a word which Quine himself has contrasted favorably with "analytic" in respect of perspicuity—the word "true." Does the indecision at once disappear? We think not. The indecision over "analytic" (and equally, in this case, the indecision over "true") arises, of course, from a further indecision: viz., that which we feel when confronted with such questions as "Should we count a *point* of green light as *extended* or not?" As is frequent enough in such cases, the hesitation arises from the fact that boundaries of application of words are not determined by usage in all possible directions. But the example Quine has chosen is particularly unfortunate for his thesis, in that it is only too evident that our hesitations are not *here* attributable to obscurities in "analytic." It would be possible to choose other examples in which we should hesitate between "analytic" and "synthetic" and have few qualms about "true." But no more in these cases than in the sample case does the hesitation necessarily imply any obscurity in the notion of analyticity; since the hesitation would be sufficiently accounted for by the same or similar kind of indeterminacy in the relations between the words occurring within the statement about which the question, whether it is analytic or synthetic, is raised.

Let us now consider briefly Quine's positive theory of the relations between the statements we accept as true or reject as false on the one hand and the "experiences" in the light of which we do this accepting and rejecting on the other. This theory is boldly sketched rather than precisely stated.[8] We shall merely extract from it two assertions, one of which Quine clearly takes to be incompatible with acceptance of the distinction between analytic and synthetic statements, and the other of which he regards as barring one way to an explanation of that distinction. We shall seek to show that the first assertion is not incompatible with acceptance of the distinction, but is, on the contrary, most intelligibly interpreted in a way quite consistent with it, and that the second assertion leaves the way open to just the kind of

8. Cf. pages 37–46.

explanation which Quine thinks it precludes. The two assertions are the following:

(1) It is an illusion to suppose that there is any class of accepted statements the members of which are in principle "immune from revision" in the light of experience, for example, any that we accept as true and must continue to accept as true whatever happens.

(2) It is an illusion to suppose that an individual statement, taken in isolation from its fellows, can admit of confirmation or disconfirmation at all. There is no particular statement such that a particular experience or set of experiences decides once for all whether that statement is true or false, independently of our attitudes to all other statements.

The apparent connection between these two doctrines may be summed up as follows. Whatever our experience may be, it is in principle possible to hold on to, or reject, any particular statement we like, so long as we are prepared to make extensive enough revisions elsewhere in our system of beliefs. In practice our choices are governed largely by considerations of convenience: we wish our system to be as simple as possible, but we also wish disturbances to it, as it exists, to be as small as possible.

The apparent relevance of these doctrines to the analytic-synthetic distinction is obvious in the first case, less so in the second.

(1) Since it is an illusion to suppose that the characteristic of immunity in principle from revision, come what may, belongs, or could belong, to any statement, it is an illusion to suppose that there is a distinction to be drawn between statements which possess this characteristic and statements which lack it. Yet, Quine suggests, this is precisely the distinction which those who use the terms "analytic" and "synthetic" suppose themselves to be drawing. Quine's view would perhaps also be (though he does not explicitly say this in the article under consideration) that those who believe in the distinction are inclined at least sometimes to mistake the characteristic of strongly resisting revision (which belongs to beliefs very centrally situated in the system) for the mythical characteristic of total immunity from revision.

(2) The connection between the second doctrine and the analytic-synthetic distinction runs, according to Quine, through the verification theory of meaning. He says: "If the verification theory can be accepted as an adequate account of statement synonymy, the notion of analyticity is saved after all." [9] For, in the first place, two statements might be said to be synonymous if and only if any experiences which contribute to, or detract from, the confirmation of one contribute to, or detract from, the confirmation of the other, to the same degree; and, in the second place, synonymy could be used to explain analyticity. But, Quine seems to argue, acceptance of any such account of synonymy can only rest on the mistaken belief that individual statements, taken in isolation from their fellows, can admit of confirmation or disconfirmation at all. As soon as we give up the idea of a set of experiential truth-conditions for each statement taken separately, we must give up the idea of explaining synonymy in terms of identity of such sets.

Now to show that the relations between these doctrines and the analytic-synthetic distinction are not as Quine supposes. Let us take the second doctrine first. It is easy to see that acceptance of the second doctrine would not compel one to abandon, but only to revise, the suggested explanation of synonymy. Quine does not deny that individual statements are regarded as confirmed or disconfirmed, are in fact rejected or accepted, in the light of experience. He denies only that these relations between single statements and experience hold independently of our attitudes to *other* statements. He means that experience can confirm or disconfirm an individual statement, only given certain assumptions about the truth or falsity of other statements. When we are faced with a "recalcitrant experience," he says, we always have a choice of what statements to amend. What we have to renounce is determined by what we are anxious to keep. This view, however, requires only a slight modification of the definition of statement synonymy in terms of confirmation and disconfirmation. All we have to say now is that two statements are synonymous if and only if any experiences which, *on certain assumptions about the truth-values of other statements,* confirm or

9. Page 38.

disconfirm one of the pair, also, *on the same assumptions,* confirm or disconfirm the other to the same degree. More generally, Quine wishes to substitute for what he conceives to be an oversimple picture of the confirmation-relations between particular statements and particular experiences, the idea of a looser relation which he call "germaneness" (p. 43). But however loosely "germaneness" is to be understood, it would apparently continue to make sense to speak of two statements as standing in the same germaneness-relation to the same particular experiences. So Quine's views are not only consistent with, but even suggest, an amended account of statement synonymy along these lines. We are not, of course, concerned to defend such an account, or even to state it with any precision. We are only concerned to show that acceptance of Quine's doctrine of empirical confirmation does not, as he says it does, entail giving up the attempt to define statement synonymy in terms of confirmation.

Now for the doctrine that there is no statement which is in principle immune from revision, no statement which might not be given up in the face of experience. Acceptance of this doctrine is quite consistent with adherence to the distinction between analytic and synthetic statements. Only, the adherent of *this* distinction must also insist on another; on the distinction between that kind of giving up which consists in merely admitting falsity, and that kind of giving up which involves changing or dropping a concept or set of concepts. Any form of words at one time held to express something true may, no doubt, at another time, come to be held to express something false. But it is not only philosophers who would distinguish between the case where this happens as the result of a change of opinion solely as to matters of fact, and the case where this happens at least partly as a result of a shift in the sense of the words. Where such a shift in the sense of the words is a necessary condition of the change in truth-value, then the adherent of the distinction will say that the form of words in question changes from expressing an analytic statement to expressing a synthetic statement. We are not now concerned, or called upon, to elaborate an adequate theory of conceptual revision, any more than we were called upon, just now, to elaborate an adequate theory of synonymy. If we can make sense of the idea that the same form of words, taken in one way (or bearing one sense), may express something true, and taken in another way (or bearing another sense), may express something false, then we can make sense of the idea of conceptual revision. And if we can make sense of this idea, then we can perfectly well preserve the distinction between the analytic and the synthetic, while conceding to Quine the revisability-in-principle of everything we say. As for the idea that the same form of words, taken in different ways, may bear different senses and perhaps be used to say things with different truth-values, the onus of showing that this is somehow a mistaken or confused idea rests squarely on Quine. The point of substance (or one of them) that Quine is making, by this emphasis on revisability, is that there is no absolute necessity about the adoption or use of any conceptual scheme whatever, or, more narrowly and in terms that he would reject, that there is no analytic proposition such that we *must* have linguistic forms bearing just the sense required to express that proposition. But it is one thing to admit this, and quite another thing to say that there are no necessities within any conceptual scheme we adopt or use, or, more narrowly again, that there are no linguistic forms which do express analytic propositions.

The adherent of the analytic-synthetic distinction may go further and admit that there may be cases (particularly perhaps in the field of science) where it would be pointless to press the question whether a change in the attributed truth-value of a statement represented a conceptual revision or not, and correspondingly pointless to press the analytic-synthetic distinction. We cannot quote such cases, but this inability may well be the result of ignorance of the sciences. In any case, the existence, if they do exist, of statements about which it is pointless to press the question of whether they are analytic or synthetic, does not entail the nonexistence of statements which are clearly classifiable in one or other of these ways and of statements our hesitation over which has different sources, such as the possibility of alternative interpretations of the linguistic forms in which they are expressed.

This concludes our examination of Quine's article. It will be evident that our purpose has been wholly negative. We have aimed to show merely that Quine's case against the existence of the analytic-synthetic distinction is not made out. His article has two parts. In one of them, the notions of the analyticity-group are criticized on the ground that they had not been adequately explained. In the other, a positive theory of truth is outlined, purporting to be incompatible with views to which believers in the analytic-synthetic distinction either must be, or are likely to be, committed. In fact, we have contended, no single point is established which those who accept the notions of the analyticity-group would feel any strain in accommodating in their own system of beliefs. This is not to deny that many of the points raised are of the first importance in connection with the problem of giving a satisfactory general account of analyticity and related concepts. We are here only criticizing the contention that these points justify the rejection, as illusory, of the analytic-synthetic distinction and the notions which belong to the same family.

# THE ANALYTIC AND THE SYNTHETIC:

## AN UNTENABLE DUALISM

### Morton G. White

*White, one of the earliest opponents of the supposed distinction between analytic statements and synthetic statements, formulates the problem much as does Quine: in the case of statements which are not analytic by virtue of their form alone, shall we explain their analyticity in terms of substituting synonyms to make them analytic in form, thereby presupposing a prior understanding of synonymy? Pointing out that he is not demanding*

From *John Dewey: Philosopher of Science and Freedom*, New York: The Dial Press, 1950. Reprinted by permission of The Dial Press and the author. For a further development of White's position see *Toward Reunion in Philosophy*, Harvard University Press, 1956, Part II.

The present paper is a revised version of one read at the annual meeting of the Fullerton Club at Bryn Mawr College on May 14, 1949. It owes its existence to the stimulus and help of Professors Nelson Goodman and W. V. Quine. My debt to them is so great that I find it hard to single out special points. My general attitude has also been influenced by discussion with Professor Alfred Tarski, although I would hesitate to attribute to him the beliefs I defend.—M.G.W.

*a synonym for 'synonym,' nor even a behavioristic criterion for it, he merely asks for a clearer understanding of synonymy, an equivalent to the term 'synonymous.' He argues that although certain statements may be stipulated as analytic according to the rules of some artificial language, it is wrong to suppose that that artificial language is the correct reconstruction of natural language. What is analytic in one artificial language may not be so in another, so they are of no help.*

*White then counterattacks two important rejoinders to the denial of the distinction between analytic and synthetic statements. The first rejoinder is the contention that analytic statements can be characterized as those statements whose denials are self-contradictory. The statements (purportedly analytic) which White is scouting do not have denials which exhibit the explicit form of a self-contradiction. The matter boils down to the feeling of horror or oddity which such denials produce. But not everybody is horrified by the same thing, and it will be necessary to separate our cases of horror at the denial of a cherished synthetic statement, and this will make the distinction a matter of degree, which is to give it up.*

*The second rejoinder is that analytic statements may be characterized as follows: analyticity accrues to 'X is Y' if we would withhold the epithet 'X' from anything which was Y. White replies that one still could not rely on distinguishing between analytic statements and firmly held synthetic statements. Lastly, White argues that the various ways which there may be to construct the criterion he seeks usually depend upon use of the contrary-to-fact conditional, which is as much wanting analysis as is analyticity.*

*There are a number of questions inspired by "The Analytic and the Synthetic: An Untenable Dualism," not all of which can be included here. For example, would not an explanation of synonymy analogous to the explanation of logical possibility undertaken by Grice and Strawson satisfy all of White's demands? They might well be unhappy to speak in terms of extensional equivalence, but they might well also invite White to investigate the actual use of phrases such as "has the same mean-*

*ing as." Indeed, how would White answer Grice and Strawson?*

*Another avenue worth exploring is White's objection to the second rejoinder. White frames his objection in terms of natives and what they would or would not say under certain circumstances. But could not the rejoinder be stronger? Would a hardy essentialist be likely to put the issue in terms of what we or the natives would or would not say? Must an essentialist put his case in terms of synonymy? And if not, could he not give an account of essential predication, and thence of analyticity, which avoids White's strictures? Lastly, it is instructive to inquire whether any of the suggested topics of discussion of "Two Dogmas of Empiricism" are relevant to "The Analytic and the Synthetic: An Untenable Dualism."*

Dewey has spent a good part of his life hunting and shooting at dualisms: body-mind, theory-practice, percept-concept, value-science, learning-doing, sensation-thought, external-internal. They are always fair game and Dewey's prose rattles with fire whenever they come into view. At times the philosophical forest seems more like a gallery at a penny arcade and the dualistic dragons move along obligingly and monotonously while Dewey picks them off with deadly accuracy. At other times we may wonder just who these monsters are. But vague as the language sometimes is, on other occasions it is suggestive, and the writer must confess to a deep sympathy with Dewey on this point. Not that distinctions ought not to be made when they are called for, but we ought to avoid making those that are unnecessary or unfounded. It is in this spirit that I wish to examine a distinction which has come to dominate so much of contemporary philosophy—the distinction between analytic and synthetic statements in one of its many forms. It must be emphasized that the views which will be put forth are not strict corollaries of Dewey's views; indeed, he sometimes deals with the question so as to suggest disagreement with what I am about to argue. But I trace the source of my own general attitudes on this point to Dewey, even though my manner and method in this paper are quite foreign to his.

Recent discussion has given evidence of dissatisfaction with the distinction between analytic and synthetic statements. A revolt seems to have developed among some philosophers who accepted this distinction as one of their basic tenets a few short years ago. So far as I know, this attitude has not been given full expression in publications, except for a few footnotes, reviews, and undeveloped asides. In this paper I want to present some of the reasons for this decline of faith in such a pivotal distinction of recent philosophy, or at least some of the reasons which have led to the decline of my own assurance. On such a matter I hesitate to name too many names, but I venture to say, under the protection of the academic freedom which still prevails on such matters, that some of my fellow revolutionaries are Professor W. V. Quine of Harvard and Professor Nelson Goodman of the University of Pennsylvania. As yet the revolution is in a fluid stage. No dictatorship has been set up, and so there is still a great deal of freedom and healthy dispute possible within the revolutionary ranks. I, for one, am drawn in this direction by a feeling that we are here faced with another one of the dualisms that Dewey has warned against.

There is some irony in the fact that some of our most severely formal logicians have played a role in creating doubt over the adequacy of this great dualism—the sharp distinction between analytic and synthetic. It is ironical because Dewey has never looked in this direction for support; indeed he has shunned it. But such a phenomenon is not rare in the history of philosophy. Dewey has told of his attachment to Hegel's language at a time when he was no longer a Hegelian, and in like manner the contemporary revolt against the distinction between analytic and synthetic may be related to Dewey's anti-dualism. Perhaps this is the pattern of philosophical progress—new wine in old bottles.

There are at least two kinds of statements which have been called analytic in recent philosophy. The first kind is illustrated by true statements of formal logic in which only logical constants and variables appear essentially, that is, logical truths in the narrowest sense. For example:

$$(p \text{ or } q) \text{ if and only if } (q \text{ or } p)$$
$$p \text{ or not-}p$$
$$\text{If } p, \text{ then not-not-}p$$

and similar truths from more advanced chapters of modern logic. With the attempts to define "analytic" as applied to these I shall not be concerned. Nor am I interested here in the ascription of analyticity to those which are derived from them by substitution of constants for variables. This does not mean that I do not have related opinions of certain philosophical characterizations of this type of statement, but rather that my main concern here is with another kind of statement usually classified as analytic.

My main worry is over what is traditionally known as essential predication, best illustrated by "All men are animals," "Every brother is a male," "All men are rational animals," "Every brother is a male sibling," "Every vixen is a fox"—Locke's *trifling propositions.* I am concerned to understand those philosophers who call such statements analytic, as opposed to true but merely synthetic statements like "All men are bipeds," "Every brother exhibits sibling rivalry," "Every vixen is cunning." The most critical kind of test occurs when we have a given predicate like "man," which is said to be analytically linked with "rational animal" but only synthetically linked with "featherless biped," although it is fully admitted that all men are in fact featherless bipeds and that all featherless bipeds are in fact men. The most critical case occurs when it is said that whereas the statement "All and only men are rational animals" is analytic, "All and only men are featherless bipeds" is true but synthetic. And what I want to understand more clearly is the ascription of analyticity in this context. What I will argue is that a number of views which have been adopted as papal on these matters are, like so many papal announcements, obscure. And what I suggest is that the pronouncements of the modern, empiricist popes are unsuccessful attempts to bolster the dualisms of medieval, scholastic popes. From the point of view of an anti-dualist, their distinctions are equally sharp, even though the moderns make the issue more linguistic in character. But the similarities between the medievals and the moderns are great; both want to preserve the distinction between essential and accidental predication and both have drawn it obscurely.

Quine [1] has formulated the problem in a convenient way. He has pointed out (with a different illustration) that the statement "Every man is a rational animal" is analytic just in case it is the result of putting synonyms for synonyms in a logical truth of the first type mentioned. Thus we have the logical truth:

(1) Every $P$ is $P$.

From which we may deduce by substitution:

(2) Every man is a man.

Now we put for the second occurrence of the word "man" the expression "rational animal" which is allegedly synonymous with it, and we have as our result:

(3) Every man is a rational animal.

We may now say that (3) is analytic in accordance with the proposed criterion. Quine has queried the phrase "logical truth" as applied to (1) and the phrase "is synonymous with" as applied to "man" and "rational animal," but I am confining myself to the latter.

Quine has said that he does not understand the term "is synonymous with" and has suggested that he won't understand it until a behavioristic criterion is presented for it. I want to begin by saying that I have difficulties with this term too, and that this is the negative plank on which our united front rests. I should say, of course, that the complaint when put this way is deceptively modest. We begin by saying we do not understand. But our opponents may counter with Dr. Johnson that they can give us arguments but not an understanding. And so it ought to be said that the objection is a little less meek; the implication is that many who *think* they understand really don't either.

Now that the problem is introduced, a few preliminary observations must be made.

First: it might be pointed out that we are searching for a synonym for the word "synonym" and we must, therefore, understand the word "synonym" to begin with. Now it *would* be pe-

1. "Notes on Existence and Necessity," *Journal of Philosophy*, 40 (1943): 113–127.

culiar to frame the thesis by saying that a synonym for "synonym" has not been found, for then it would appear as if I did not understand the word "synonym." Obviously, if I did not understand the word "synonym" and I formulated my complaint in this way, I could hardly be said to understand my own complaint. But such criticism is avoided by saying, not that there is no synonym available for the word "synonym," but rather that no one has presented even an extensional equivalent of it which is clearer than it. In short, rather weak demands are made on those who hold that the word "synonym" may be used in clearing up "analytic"; they are merely asked to present a criterion, another term which is extensionally equivalent to "synonym." In other words, a term which bears the relation to "synonym" that "featherless biped" bears to "man" on their view.

Second: whereas Quine appears to require that the criterion for being synonymous be behavioristic or at least predicts that he won't understand it if it's not, I make less stringent demands. The term formulating the criterion of being synonymous will satisfy me if I understand it more clearly than I understand the term "synonymous" now. And I don't venture conditions any more stringent than that. It should be said in passing that Quine's behaviorism would appear quite consonant with Dewey's general views.

Third: it is obvious that if the problem is set in the manner outlined, then the statement " 'All men are rational animals' is analytic" is itself empirical. For to decide that the statement is analytic we will have to find out whether "man" is in fact synonymous with "rational animal" and this will require the empirical examination of linguistic usage. This raises a very important problem which helps us get to the root of the difficulty and to ward off one very serious misunderstanding.

The demonstration that "All men are rational animals" is analytic depends on showing that it is the result of putting a synonym for its synonym in a logical truth. In this situation we find ourselves asking whether a statement in a natural language or what Moore calls ordinary language—a language which has not been formalized by a logician—is analytic. We find ourselves asking whether two expressions in a natural language are synonymous. But this must be distinguished from a closely related situation. It must be distinguished from the case where we artificially construct a language and propose so-called definitional rules. In this case we are not faced with the same problem. Obviously we may *decide* to permit users of our language to put "rational animal" for "man" in a language $L_1$. (For the moment I will not enter the question of how this decision is to be formulated precisely.) In that same language, $L_1$, which also contains the phrase "featherless biped" in its vocabulary, there may be no rule permitting us to put "featherless biped" for "man." Thus we may say that in artificial language $L_1$ "All men are rational animals" is analytic on the basis of a convention, a rule explicitly stated. In $L_1$, moreover, "All men are featherless bipeds" is not analytic. But it is easy to see that we can construct a language $L_2$ in which the reverse situation prevails and in which a linguistic shape which was analytic in $L_1$ becomes synthetic in $L_2$, etc.

Now no one denies that two such languages can be constructed having the features outlined. But these languages are the creatures of formal fancy; they are dreamed up by a logician. If I ask: "Is 'All men are rational animals' analytic in $L_1$?" I am rightly told to look up the rule-book of language $L_1$.[2] But natural languages have no rule-books and the question of whether a given statement is analytic in them is much more difficult. We know that dictionaries are not very helpful on this matter. What some philosophers do is to pretend that natural languages are really quite like these artificial languages; and that even though there is no rule-book for them, people do behave *as if* there were such a book. What some philosophers usually assume is that the artificial rule-book which they construct in making an artificial language is the rule-book which ordinary people or scientists *would* construct, if they were asked to construct one, or that it is the rule-book which, in that vague phrase, presents *the* rational reconstruction of the usage in question. But suppose a logician constructs $L_1$ and $L_2$ as defined above, and now suppose he approaches $L_3$, a natural language, with them. Can he say in any

2. Even here, Quine asks, how do you know a rule when you see one? Only by the fact that the book has the word "Rule-Book" on it, he answers.

clear way that $L_1$ is *the* rational reconstruction of $L_3$ and that $L_2$ is not? My whole point is that no one has been able to present the criterion for such claims. And the reason for this is that no one has succeeded in finding a criterion for synonymy.

The moral of this is important for understanding the new revolt against dualism. I hope it makes clear that whereas I understand fairly well the expressions "analytic in $L_1$" and "analytic in $L_2$," where $L_1$ and $L_2$ are the artificial languages mentioned, I do not understand as well the phrase "analytic in the natural language $L_3$." [3] More important to realize is that my understanding of the first two expressions in no way solves the serious problem of analyticity as I conceive it, and I want to repeat that my major difficulties will disappear only when a term is presented which is coextensive with "synonymous" and on the basis of which I can (operationally, if you like) distinguish analytic sheep from synthetic goats. I want to repeat that I am not doing anything as quixotic as seeking a synonym for "synonym."

Those who refuse to admit the distinction between "analytic in $L_1$" and "analytic in the natural language $L_3$" will, of course, disagree completely. But then, it seems to me, they will have to refrain from attributing analyticity to any statement which has not been codified in a formalized language. In which case they will find it hard to do analysis in connection with terms in *ordinary language*. They may say, as I have suggested, that people using natural languages behave *as if* they had made rules for their language just like those of $L_1$ and $L_2$, but then how do we establish when people behave *as if* they had done something which they haven't done? As we shall see later, clearing up this problem is just as difficult as the one we start with, for it involves the equally vexations problem of contrary-to-fact conditional statements. I suppose it would be granted that those who use natural language do not make conventions and rules of definition by making a linguistic contract at the dawn of history. What defenders of the view I am criticizing want to hold, however, is that there are other ways of finding out whether a group of people has a convention. And what I am saying is that phi-

---

3. For many years Quine has also pointed to the unclarity of the phrase "analytic in L," where "L" is a variable even over formal languages.

losophers should tell us what these ways are before they dub statements in natural languages "analytic" and "synthetic."

The point at issue is closely related to one discussed at length by Professor C. I. Lewis in *An Analysis of Knowledge and Valuation* (1946). We agree in seeing a problem here which is overlooked by what I shall call crude conventionalism, but differ in our conception of where the solution must be sought. Lewis is led to say that whether "All men are rational animals" is analytic in a natural language depends on whether all men are necessarily rational animals, and this in turn depends on whether the *criterion in mind* of *man* includes the *criterion in mind* of *rational animal*. Lewis has dealt with this matter more extensively than any recent philosopher who advocates a sharp distinction between analytic and synthetic, and his arguments are too complex to be treated here. In any case, his views are quite different from those upon which I am concentrating in this paper. He holds that I need only make what he calls an "experiment in imagination" to find out whether all men are necessarily rational animals. And when I try this experiment I am supposed to conclude that I *cannot* consistently think of, that I cannot conceive of, a man who is not a rational animal. But how shall we interpret this "cannot"? How shall we understand "thinkable"? I suspect that this view leads us to a private, intuitive insight for determining what each of us individually *can* conceive. How, then, can we get to the analyticity of the *commonly* understood statement? Lewis' most helpful explanation turns about the word 'include' in the following passage: "The question, 'Does your schematism for determining application of the term *"square"* include your schematism for applying *"rectangle"*?' is one determined in the same general fashion as is the answer to the question, 'Does your plan of a trip to Chicago to see the Field Museum include the plan of visiting Niagara to see the Falls?'" The inclusion of plans, furthermore, is a sense-apprehensible relationship for Lewis. One either sees or doesn't see the relationship and that is the end of the matter. It is very difficult to argue one's difficulties with such a position and I shall only say dogmatically that I do not find this early retreat to intuition satisfactory. I will add, however, that in its recognition of the problem Lewis' view is closer to the one advanced in this paper than those which do not see the need for clarification of "analytic in natural language." My difficulties with Professor Lewis are associated with the difficulties of intensionalism but that is a large matter.

I want to consider now two views which are avowedly anti-intensional and more commonly held by philosophers against whom my critical comments are primarily directed.

1—*"Analytic statements are those whose denials are self-contradictory."* Consider this criterion as applied to the contention that "All men are rational animals" is analytic in a natural language. We are invited to take the denial of this allegedly analytic statement, namely "It is not the case that all men are rational animals." But is this a self-contradiction? Certainly looking at it syntactically shows nothing like "*A and not-A.*" And even if we transform it into "Some men are not rational animals" we still do not get a self-contradiction in the syntactical form. It might be said that the last statement is self-contradictory *in the sense* in which "man" is being used. But surely the phrase "in the sense" is a dodge. Because if he is asked to specify that sense, what can the philosopher who has referred to it say? Surely not "the sense in which 'man' is synonymous with 'rational animal'" because that would beg the question. The point is that the criterion under consideration is not helpful if construed literally and if not construed literally (as in the attempt to use the phrase "in the sense") turns out to beg the question.

Let us then suppose that the criterion is not used in this question-begging manner. A self-contradiction need not literally resemble in shape "*A and not-A*" or "Something is *P* and not-*P.*" All it has to do is to produce a certain feeling of horror or queerness on the part of people who use the language. They behave as if they had seen someone eat peas with a knife. Such an approach is very plausible and I would be satisfied with an account of the kind of horror or queer feelings which people are supposed to have in the presence of the denials of analytic statements. But on this I have a few questions and observations. (a) Who is supposed to feel the horror in the presence of the opposites of analytic statements? Surely not all people in the community that uses the language. There are many who feel no horror at seeing people eat peas with a knife just as there are many who are not perturbed at statements that philosophers might think self-contradictory. Who, then?

(b) Let us remember that on this view we will have to be careful to distinguish the horror associated with denying firmly believed synthetic statements from that surrounding the denials of analytic statements. The distinction must not only be a distinction that carves out two mutually exclusive classes of sentences but it must carve them out in a certain way. It would be quite disconcerting to these philosophers to have the whole of physics or sociology turn out as analytic on their criterion and only a few parts of mathematics.

(c) If analytic statements are going to be distinguished from synthetic true statements on the basis of the degree of discomfort that is produced by denying them, the distinction will not be a sharp one [4] and the current rigid separation of analytic and synthetic will have been surrendered. The dualism will have been surrendered, and the kind of *gradualism* one finds in Dewey's writings will have been vindicated. The most recent justification of the distinction between essential and accidental predication will have been refuted. It may be said that sharp differences are compatible with matters of degree. Differences of temperature are differences of degree and yet we may mark fixed points like 0° centigrade on our thermometers. But it should be pointed out that a conception according to which "analytic" is simply the higher region of a scale on which "synthetic" is the lower region, breaks down the radical separation of the analytic and the synthetic as expressive of different kinds of knowledge. And this is a great concession from the view that K. R. Popper [5] calls "essentialism." It is reminiscent of the kind of concession that Mill wanted to wrest from the nineteenth century in connection with the status of arithmetical statements. Once it is admitted that analytic statements are just like synthetic statements, only

4. On this point see Nelson Goodman's "On Likeness of Meaning," in *Analysis* (October 1949), pp. 1–7. Also W. V. Quine's *Methods of Logic,* sec. 33 (Henry Holt, N.Y., 1950).

5. See *The Open Society and Its Enemies,* especially ch. 11 and its notes (Routledge, London, 1945).

that they produce a little more of a certain quality—in this case the quality of discomfort in the presence of their denials—the bars are down, and a radical, gradualistic pragmatism is enthroned. This is the kind of enthronement which the present writer would welcome.

2—"*If we were presented with something which wasn't a rational animal, we would not call it a man.*" Such language is often used by philosophers who are anxious to clarify the notion of analytic in the natural languages. In order to test its effectiveness in distinguishing analytic statements let us try it on "All men are featherless bipeds" which by hypothesis is *not* analytic. Those who use this criterion would have to deny that if we were presented with an entity which was not a biped or not featherless we would not call it a man. But we *do* withhold the term "man" from those things which we know to be either non-bipeds or non-featherless. Obviously everything turns about the phrase "we would not call it a man" or the phrase "we would withhold the term 'man.'" Again, who are we? And more important, what is the pattern of term-withholding? Suppose I come to a tribe which has the following words in its vocabulary plus a little logic: "man," "rational," "animal," "featherless," and "biped." I am told in advance by previous visiting anthropologists that "man" is synonymous with "rational animal'" in that tribe's language, whereas "featherless biped" is merely coextensive with it. I wish to check the report of the anthropologists. How do I go about it?

In the spirit of the proposed criterion I must show that if anything lacked rationality it would not be reputed a man by the people in question. So I show them cocoanuts, trees, horses, pigs, and I ask after each "man?" and get "no" for an answer. They will not repute these things to be men. I must now show that there is a difference in their attitudes toward "rational animal" and "featherless biped" *vis-a-vis* "man." I originally produced things which lacked rational animality. But these very things also lack feathers and are not bipeds, and so the negative responses of the natives might just as well be offered as an argument for the synonymy of "man" and "featherless biped" as for the theory that "man" is synonymous with "rational animal." It

would appear that such crude behaviorism will not avail. They
don't call non-featherless-bipeds men just as they don't call non-
rational-animals men. The criterion, therefore, is one that will
not help us make the distinction.

We might pursue the natives in another way. We might ask
them: Would you call something a man if it were not a featherless biped? To which they answer in the negative. Would you
call something a man if it weren't a rational animal? To which
they answer "no" again. But now we might ask them: Aren't
your reasons different in each of these cases?—hoping to lead
them into saying something that will allow us to differentiate
their responses. Aren't you surer in concluding that something is
not a man from the fact that it is not a rational animal, than you
are in concluding it from the fact that it is not a featherless
biped? If the savage is obliging and says "yes," we have the
making of a criterion. But notice that it is a criterion which
makes of the distinction a matter of degree. Not being a rational
animal is simply a better sign of the absence of manhood than
is the property of not being a featherless biped, just as the latter
is a better sign than the property of not wearing a derby hat. It
should be noticed in this connection that we are precluded from
saying that the inference from "*a* is not a rational animal" to "*a* is
not a man" is logical or analytic for them, since we are trying to
explain "analytic." To use it in the explanation would hardly be
helpful.

Probably the most helpful interpretation of this mode of distinguishing analytic and synthetic is that according to which we
observe the following: when the natives have applied the word
"man" to certain objects and are then persuaded that these objects are not rational animals, they immediately, without hesitation, withdraw the predicate "man." They contemplate no other
means of solving their problem. But when they have applied the
word "man" and are then persuaded that the things to which
they have applied it are not featherless bipeds, they do not withdraw the predicate "man" immediately but rather contemplate
another course, that of surrendering the hypothesis that all men
are featherless bipeds. Now I suspect that this criterion will be
workable but it will not allow us to distinguish what we think

in advance are the analytic equivalences. It will result in our finding that many firmly believed "synthetic" equivalences are analytic on this criterion.

I am sure that there are a number of other ways of constructing the criterion that are similar to the ones I have just considered. No doubt students of language who have thought of this problem can develop them. But I want to call attention to one general problem that criteria of this sort face. They usually depend on the use of the contrary-to-fact conditional: if . . . were . . . then . . . would be. . . . But in appealing to this (or any variety of causal conditional) we are appealing to a notion which is just as much in need of explanation as the notion of *analytic* itself. To appeal to it, therefore, does not constitute a philosophical advance. Goodman [6] has reported on the lugubrious state of this notion, if there are some who are not fazed by this circumstance. It would be small consolation to reduce "analytic" to the contrary-to-fact conditional, for that is a very sandy foundation right now.

After presenting views like these I frequently find philosophers agreeing with me. Too often they are the very philosophers whose views I had supposed I was criticizing. Too often, I find, the criticisms I have leveled are treated as arguments *for* what I had supposed I was opposing. For example, there are some philosophers who construe the argument merely as an argument to show that words in natural language and scientific language are ambiguous—that "man" is synonymous with "rational animal" in one situation and with "featherless biped" in another— and who immediately embrace the views here set forth. But this is not what is being emphasized. Many philosophers who defend the view I have criticized admit that a word may have many meanings, depending on context. For example, John Stuart Mill, who admits that a biologist might regard as a synonym of "man," "mammiferous animal having two hands," and not "rational animal." But Mill also holds that in common usage "rational animal" is the synonym. Because of this admission of a varying connotation Mill regards himself (justifiably) as superior to the

6. "The Problem of Counterfactual Conditionals," *Journal of Philosophy*, 44 (1947), 113–128.

benighted philosopher who holds what has been called "The one and only one true meaning" view of analysis. If the benighted philosopher is asked "What is the synonym of 'man'?" he immediately replies "rational animal." If he is a Millian, he says it depends on the situation in which it is used, etc.

I am not concerned to advocate this view here, because it is quite beside the point so far as the thesis of this paper is concerned. The difference between the Millian (if I may call him that without intending thereby to credit Mill with having originated the view) and his opponent (I would call him an Aristotelian if such matters were relevant) is comparatively slight. The Millian takes as his fundamental metalinguistic statement-form: "$X$ is synonymous with $Y$ in situation $S$," where as his opponent apparently refuses to relativize synonymy. The opponent merely says: "$X$ is synonymous with $Y$." What I want to emphasize, however, is that by so relativizing the notion of synonymy he is still far from meeting the difficulty I have raised. For now it may be asked how we establish synonymy *even in a given situation*. The problem is analogous to the following one in mechanics. Suppose one holds that the question: "Is $x$ moving?" is unanswerable before a frame of reference is given. Suppose, then, that motion is relativized and we now ask such questions in the form: "Is $x$ moving with respect to $y$?" But now suppose we are not supplied with a clear statement of how to go about finding out whether $x$ is in motion with respect to $y$. I venture to say that the latter predicament resembles that of philosophers who are enlightened enough to grant that synonymy is relative to a linguistic context, but who are unable to see that even when relativized it still needs more clarification than anyone has given it.

I think that the problem is clear, and that all considerations point to the need for dropping the myth of a sharp distinction between essential and accidental predication (to use the language of the *older* Aristotelians) as well as its contemporary formulation—the sharp distinction between analytic and synthetic. I am not arguing that a criterion of analyticity and synonymy can never be given. I argue that none has been given and, more positively, that a suitable criterion is likely to make the distinction between analytic and synthetic a matter of degree. If this is tenable, then a dualism which has been shared by both scholastics and empiricists will have been challenged successfully. Analytic philosophy will no longer be sharply separated from science, and an unbridgeable chasm will no longer divide those who see meanings or essences and those who collect facts. Another revolt against dualism will have succeeded.

# SYNONYMITY

## Benson Mates

*Mates treats so many matters in his article that there is simply not enough space to give a fair, detailed summary. Rather, we shall simply mark two relevant features of the article, and leave the rest to the reader. Quine's article, it will be recalled, was designed in part to question the notion of synonymy. And the question is whether Mates already may have supplied a satisfactory explanation of that notion. Mates, it should be noted, is writing before the appearance of "Two Dogmas."*

*A part of Mates' total strategy is to propose and defend an account of synonymy, although he does not pretend to have defined that notion. This introduces the first point to be marked. For Mates proposes interchangeability salva veritate as an account of synonymy. In his own words: "Two expressions are synonymous in a language L if and only if they may be inter-*

From the *University of California Publications in Philosophy*, 25 (1950). Reprinted by permission of University of California Press and the author.

*changed in each sentence in L without altering the truth of that sentence." The reader will note the great care with which Mates nominates interchangeability. Noting that if two expressions are synonymous they will be interchangeable, Mates goes on to the more difficult matter as to whether interchangeability guarantees synonymy. Using modal and psychological contexts where interchangeability salva veritate often fails, he argues that synonymy is necessary to guarantee interchangeability in such contexts. He goes on to say that considerations similar to those which proved this last result will show that if two expressions are not synonymous, they will not be interchangeable. Thus, in languages rich enough to contain modal contexts and indirect discourse, Mates argues, his condition for synonymy holds. For languages not this rich, any two logically equivalent expressions will turn out to be synonymous, but this conforms to Mates' condition, even though this does some violence to our everyday notion of synonymy.*

*There is much more of interest in Mates' article. But even in the small part of it that we have been able to consider here, intriguing questions arise. For example, there is the question whether, in a language containing both modal contexts and indirect discourse, there are any synonyms at all. Ignorance, either of language or of fact, would seem capable of breaking any claim of synonymy. Indeed, this situation might well occur in languages which lack modal contexts but which contain indirect discourse. Moreover, it is questionable whether Mates' condition can be used to solve Quine's problem. For, insofar as modality is used in the characterization of Mates' condition, so, in Quine's view, is the notion of analyticity tacitly presupposed. And there remains the question as to how much violence to our notion of synonymy in extensional languages can be tolerated. Even when the notion of synonymy is relativized to the language at hand, are we really to say that 'scrofula' and 'the king's evil' are synonymous because they are everywhere interchangeable? (Since the language at hand is an extensional one.) In other words, does the Mates condition provide for synonymy in either extensional or non-extensional languages? Another avenue of inquiry leads to the question of subjectivity. Can 'shingles' and 'herpes zoster' be synonymous for the knowledgeable Jed, and not for poor Ned, who has never heard the latter expression? Does synonymy fail if we can find just one such creature as Ned? Is it then a matter of richness of vocabulary that is at least partly involved? These are some questions prompted by the Mates condition. How fruitful they are is up to the reader to decide.*

# I

I shall begin my paper by attempting to show, in a rough way at least, that a discussion of synonymity is germane to the general topic of these lectures, namely, meaning and interpretation. The connection between synonymity and meaning is perhaps too clear to require much comment: two linguistic expressions are synonymous if and only if they have the same meaning. The relation between synonymity and interpretation is only slightly less obvious. I shall try to explicate it by offering definitions of certain important terms which commonly occur, or ought to occur, in discussions of this subject.

The first of these terms is "language." By "language," in its most general sense, I wish to denote any aggregate of objects which are themselves meaningful or else are such that certain combinations of them are meaningful. It will be seen at once that this definition assigns a very wide meaning to the term "language" and furthermore that it suffers from all the vagueness and ambiguity which attach to the word "meaningful." Nevertheless, I think that it leads to a usage quite in agreement with ordinary usage. Thus we may first of all observe that all the ordinary conversational languages, for example the English language or the German, come under the definition given. Each of them can be regarded as an aggregate of objects which are meaningful singly or at least in combination. Likewise, written English, spoken English, the King's English, and plain English would all be languages according to the definition just given.

As one can determine by consulting the dictionary, however, the denotation of the word "language" is much wider than these examples indicate. We must not suppose, for instance, that only human beings can use language, since in one proper sense of the term it refers to activities of the lower animals as well. For example, there is said to be a "language of the birds." Here the meaningful objects are the various characteristic sounds that birds make under given circumstances. Nor, again, must we suppose that the elements of a language are always either inscriptions or sounds. There is, for instance, "the language of the face," or "the language of looks and glances." In this case the meaningful elements are evidently certain positions of the physiognomy. Again, the phrase "language of the heart" presumably refers to a language whose elements are certain patterns of behavior which are supposed to denote the presence of certain emotions. But even these examples do not show the full extent of the term "language" in ordinary discourse. It is by no means necessary that the elements of the language be the results of human or animal activity. Thus, certain clever men are said to be able to read "the language of the stars," and poets and philosophers have a great deal to say about "the language of nature." What is common to all these, it seems to me, is that in each there is an aggregate of objects—whether they be marks, sounds, gestures, looks, or stars—and these objects or certain combinations of these objects are meaningful.

The next important term for which I shall offer a preliminary definition is the term "translation." A body of discourse A is a translation of another body of discourse B if and only if there is a correspondence between the meaningful parts of A and those of B such that corresponding parts are synonymous. What kind of correspondence this is, in general, it is difficult to say. At present, I am merely trying to indicate the connection between the notions of translation and synonymity, and I claim for the foregoing definition only the merit that its consequences are to a great extent in accord with the ordinary usage of the word "translation." Consider, for example, the problem of translating a book from German into English. This amounts to the problem of producing an English version which faithfully reproduces the sense of the original, that is, of producing a book which contains, for every meaningful expression in the German original, a synonymous expression in English, and conversely. Words, sentences, or whole paragraphs may be taken as the smallest meaningful expressions to be translated, depending upon the translator's judgment of how the sense of the original can best be reproduced in the translation.[1]

The term "translation" is most frequently applied when the two texts occur in languages that are entirely disjoint from one another, as for example German and English. However, it may equally well be applied when one of the two languages is contained in the other or even when the two languages are identical. Consider the task of popularizing a technical treatise—of putting it into plain English. It seems to me that the popularization will be a translation of the technical treatise in essentially the same sense in which a German version would be a translation of it. We are given a language—German, or plain English, as the case may be—and the problem is to find, for every expression or group of expressions in the technical treatise, a synonymous expression or group of expressions in the given language. The process of popularization, therefore, may be regarded as a process of translating the technical treatise out of the whole English language (considered as containing the technical terms) into that part of the English language which we have been calling "plain English." It may also occur that the languages concerned are identical or nearly so. For example, it is perfectly in accord with correct usage to speak of translating poetry into prose. Here the problem is to find nonpoetic expressions which are synonymous with the meaningful expressions occurring in some poem, and both the poem and the prose may of course be written in the same language.

The last term for which I shall give a preliminary definition is "interpretation." A body of discourse A is an interpretation of a body of discourse B if and only if A is a translation of B and the constituent expressions of A are better understood than those of B. Thus, according to me, every interpretation is a translation.[2]

---

1. In general we may say that a translation is relatively literal if it is so constructed that for every important word in the original text there is a synonymous expression in the translation, while it would be considered relatively free if whole paragraphs were the smallest parts for which synonymous expressions were provided.

2. I do not think that the interpretation of calculi is a type of interpretation under discussion in these lectures; at any rate, I have not attempted to define "interpretation" in such a way as to cover that usage of the term.

Further, since the degree to which a language is understood varies from person to person, what would be an interpretation for one person might not be an interpretation for someone else.

I shall now set forth a series of considerations which will serve both to explain my definition of "interpretation" and to argue that it accords well with established usage. Let us first give attention to the meaning of the related term, "interpret." We may say that a person $x$ interprets a given body of discourse A to a person $y$ if and only if $x$ translates A into a body of discourse which $y$ understands better than he understands A. This general statement obviously holds when the languages concerned are ordinary natural languages, for example French and German; and indeed the term "interpreter" is ordinarily applied to a person who translates discourse from one such language into another for the benefit of someone who is not able to understand the first. But it is equally true that the statement holds when the languages concerned are systems of meaningful objects of any sort whatever. To interpret a poem for someone is usually to translate the poem into linguistic expressions which he can understand better than he understands the poem. Sometimes the translator may find it desirable to use gestures, signs, tears, and other devices in addition to the meaningful expressions of the conversational language. We shall then regard the language into which the translation is made as a rather complex language, consisting not only of written or spoken expressions but also of these various other occurrences. In like manner the astrologer may properly be said to interpret the positions of the heavenly bodies. He and his clients regard the positions of these objects as meaningful symbols, that is, as elements in a language which the astrologer can understand but the clients cannot. His function is to interpret discourse in this language to the others, which is to say, to translate messages out of the language of the heavens into a language which the others can understand.[3]

3. It is interesting and important to observe that even though the clientele do not understand the language of the stars, it is quite possible for them to determine that they have not been provided with an adequate interpretation. It is to be assumed, of course, that the pronouncements of the stars are true; hence, any adequate translation of these pronouncements must at least consist of true sentences. Thus the astrology business is not quite as safe as it might at first seem to be.

Almost all the other situations which would ordinarily be regarded as instances of interpretation will satisfy the definition proposed above. When the psychiatrist interprets dreams he treats the dreams or certain important constituents of them as meaningful expressions in a kind of language which he, by means of a great deal of training, finds it possible to understand. He is able to tell the uninitiated person what the dreams mean, that is, he can translate certain significant elements in what we may call "the language of dreams" into sentences occurring in a more readily intelligible language. Likewise, the person who interprets a painting regards the painting and possibly also various parts of it as somehow meaningful, and he attempts by the use of the meaningful expressions of some language, usually supplemented by an assortment of meaningful gestures, and so on, to accomplish a translation of the painting into forms of expression which are more readily understandable to the person for whose benefit the interpretation is made.

As I see it, therefore, most situations to which the word "interpretation" can properly be applied have the following characteristics. First of all, there are two bodies of discourse, which may occur in any language or languages, in the broad sense of "language" explained above. Secondly, there is a person who understands only one of these bodies of discourse, which is to say that the constituent expressions of only one of these bodies of discourse are meaningful for him. This is the person for whose benefit the interpretation is carried out. Thirdly, there is a person who understands both bodies of discourse and who is able to translate one into the other. This person is the interpreter. Finally we set these elements in motion: the interpreter translates the discourse which the other person does not understand into discourse which the other person does understand. This is interpretation, considered as a process; and the result of the translation is the interpretation, considered as a product.

There is an important difficulty which ought to be mentioned at this point. It very often happens that when an interpretation is needed there is no capable interpreter at hand to produce it. Any student of the history of philosophy will, unfortunately, be well acquainted with this difficulty; but of course the same situation arises in fields other than philosophy. For example, in war-time we may possess enemy messages in code or cipher but lack a ready means of translating these messages into plain language. If an interpretation is to be found at all, it will be necessary for someone who does not understand the text to make an interpretation for himself. Often this is no easy task, but we know that it can be done. In cryptanalysis the methods which are used depend essentially upon the fact that an adequate interpretation of the cryptic message will be part-by-part synonymous with the cryptic message; hence, if the cryptic message is about battle-ships, the interpretation must be about battleships; if the cryptic message contains true sentences, the interpretation must contain true sentences; if the cryptic message expresses information that would be of interest to the persons for whom it was intended, the interpretation must likewise express information that would interest those persons, and so forth. Thus by the use of data concerning the circumstances under which the message was sent, together with further data about the methods likely to have been used by the cryptographer who wrote the message, it is possible to arrive at a probable interpretation. It is clear that similar considerations enable us to find more or less probable interpretations for obscure passages in philosophical discourse. We know that an adequate interpretation would preserve sense; this requires that it take true sentences over into true ones and false into false; it also requires that valid arguments be interpreted by valid arguments, and invalid arguments by invalid ones. Usually we also possess some knowledge of the rules of syntax for the language in which the obscure passage is stated; here we have a great advantage over the cryptanalyst. For example, we may often safely assume that, within limits, a given expression should always be translated by the same expression. Frequently we have also a good deal of other knowledge about our author's views and capability, and often we have the opinions of other men on how the passage should be interpreted. By means of all these data we construct a more or less adequate interpretation.

I shall now try to anticipate all the objections which may be made to the foregoing definition of "interpretation," but there are two points which I am prompted to set forth. In the first place, although the definition offered above leads to a very broad usage of "interpretation," it requires that interpretation be sharply distinguished from description. This will appear clearly in an example. Suppose that Jones is an interpreter for the Army in Germany. The prisoner, looking out the window, remarks, "Es schneit," and Jones is asked for an interpretation. He replies as follows: "He uttered a German sentence consisting of two words, the first of which was 'es' and the second, 'schneit.'" I think we may confidently say that although Jones has even given a description of what was said, he has certainly not given an adequate interpretation of what was said. This case is typical; in general, a description of an aggregate of objects is by no means the same as an interpretation of those objects. Thus, even if it could be shown that it is impossible to report what one perceives without describing something, it would not follow that it is impossible to report what one perceives without interpreting something.

The second point which I wish to make is this: from the earliest times, men have tended to confuse interpretation with explanation. If we believe in progress, we shall say that this confusion was more prevalent in ancient times than it is now. At any rate, it will be less offensive to illustrate the matter in connection with antiquity. The history of natural philosophy in the ancient world shows that attempts to explain natural phenomena took two easily distinguishable forms. Sometimes the explanations were explanations in the scientific sense of the term; that is, from a relatively well-established generalization there was deduced a sentence expressing the state of affairs to be explained. More often, however, the explanations were what we would call "interpretations." The phenomenon to be explained was regarded as possessing a meaning with which it had been endowed by some supernatural being, and the explanation consisted in reading off this meaning. Thus, for example, some would explain an eclipse of the sun by saying, "The gods are displeased with men"; others by saying, "The moon has come between the earth and the sun." The former explanation seems based on the assumption that the eclipse is a meaningful symbol by which the gods intend to reveal their displeasure. This sort of explanation might better be called "interpretation," it seems to me.[4] The naturalistic explanation, on the other hand, does not rest upon any assumption that the eclipse is a symbol or portent which the gods or anyone else has endowed with meaning. It corresponds more exactly to what would now be denoted by the word "explanation." There were thus two quite distinct types of explanation, one of which was a type of interpretation and one of which was not. This may account for some of the present-day confusion between the notions of interpretation and explanation and for much of the ambiguity in the English word "interpretation."

## II

The preceding section has shown that the notion of synonymity is involved in the notions of meaning and interpretation. The question which naturally arises is, "What can be offered by way of a definition of 'synonymity'?" From what has been said it appears that if one could find a precise and plausible definition for this term, then it would be a relatively simple matter to construct satisfactory definitions for the other important terms which we have been discussing. That circumstance alone would make explicating the notion of synonymity a worthwhile task for philosophers, but it is also true that the notion deserves to be investigated in its own right because of the key role which it plays in many philosophical discussions. This key role is often disguised through the fact that there are many different ways of saying that two expressions are synonymous. One group of circumlocutions consists of those having the form 'to say A is only to say B'; [5] for example, "if by 'good' you mean pleasure, then to say that

4. In fact, it *was* called *interpretatio* by the ancients. Thus, Mercury was called *interpres divum*—interpreter of things divine—because he understood the decrees of Jove and Apollo, not to mention a wide assortment of other omens, including the tripods, laurel, and stars, as well as the sounds (*linguas*) and flights of birds. See Virgil, *Aeneid*, 4, 356; 3, 359.

5. Single quotation marks, when they enclose expressions containing variables, are to be regarded as quasi-quotation marks. See W. V. Quine, *Mathematical Logic* (New York, Norton, 1940), pp. 33 ff.

pleasure is good is only to say that pleasure is pleasure." Another way of claiming synonymity is to use expressions like 'A; in other words, B'—for instance, "Jones is a positivist; in other words, Jones regards the sentences of metaphysics as pseudo-object sentences." Still other ways make use of the formula 'when I say A, I only mean B,' and there are further types too numerous to mention. The notion of synonymity seems also to be involved in the well-worn notions of analytic and synthetic sentences, real definitions, analysis, and in much of the other conceptual apparatus of philosophers. Thus there is no doubt that this notion, however vague it may be, is of considerable philosophical importance, and a good definition of it is greatly to be desired.[6]

This being so, the appropriate thing for me to do is to produce such a definition or at least to make an attempt to do so. I am sorry to have to confess not only that I have no definition to propose but also that it seems to me doubtful that any adequate definition of "synonymity"—at least for languages sufficiently complex to make the problem interesting—will ever be found by means of the usual armchair methods of philosophizing. We need empirical research regarding the ordinary language in order to determine which expressions are in fact synonymous, and with the help of these data it may be possible to find an acceptable definition of "synonymity" for some language which has a determinate structure and which closely resembles the ordinary language.

Yet it is important to observe that this very research could hardly be carried out unless we possessed in advance a sufficiently precise characterization of synonymity to enable us to decide under what conditions we would regard two expressions as synonymous for a given person. Otherwise, we would be forced to ask questions of the form 'Are A and B synonymous?'; and the answers would depend not only upon whether or not the subjects regarded the expressions as synonymous, but also upon how they understood the term "synonymous." The case is analogous to the following. Suppose that we wanted to determine

6. As I use the terms, "to find a plausible definition of the term," "to explicate the notion," and "to define the notion" denote the same process.

whether John Smith is color-blind. We would not do this by asking him the question, "Are you color-blind?" for his answers would depend upon how *he* interpreted the term "color-blind," whereas we wish to know whether he is color-blind in *our* sense of the term. Consequently, we would ask such questions as "Do you see a number on this page?" and would employ some such criterion as "Smith is color-blind if and only if he does not see the number '7' on this page of the text book." In the same way, we need a criterion of the form 'A and B are synonymous if and only if . . .' in order to be able to investigate which terms are actually synonymous.

Accordingly, I propose the following statement as a condition of adequacy for definitions of "synonymity" and as a guide for conducting research to determine which expressions are in fact synonymous for given persons: *Two expressions are synonymous in a language L if and only if they may be interchanged in each sentence in L without altering the truth-value of that sentence.* That we ordinarily intend to use the word "synonymity" in such a way as to satisfy this condition will be argued in the sequel; first, allow me to make two remarks concerning its application. It is plain, no doubt, that this condition refers only to synonymity between expressions which occur in the same language. We shall need a different and more general criterion for the synonymity of expressions occurring in different languages.[7] Secondly, I intend this condition to apply only to languages which are not semantically closed, that is, to languages which do not contain names of their own expressions and semantical terms like "true," "denotes," and so forth. In particular, it is important that the language L not contain the semantical term "synonymous in L."

It is easy to see that if two expressions are synonymous in a language L, then they may be interchanged in any sentence in L

7. I assume that we are dealing with a language in which the formation rules do not prevent the interchange of expressions of the same type. Thus, the fact that "humanity" and "human" are not interchangeable in English does not indicate a difference in meaning, for syntax alone prevents their interchange. Now although the union of two languages is always a language, it is not generally the case that the union of two languages of the sort under consideration is a language of the sort under consideration. This is why we shall need a different criterion for the synonymity of expressions occurring in different languages.

without altering the truth-value of that sentence. For, following Frege, we may say that the meaning of a sentence is a function of the meanings of the terms which occur in the sentence; from this it follows that if, in a given sentence, we replace a term by an expression which is synonymous with that term, then the resulting sentence is synonymous with (has the same meaning as) the original sentence. Further, it is clear that synonymous sentences have the same truth-value. Hence, synonymous expressions may be interchanged without affecting the meaning or truth-value of sentences in which they occur.

Next, it requires to be shown that, if two expressions can be interchanged in each sentence in L without altering the truth-value of that sentence, then they are synonymous. Let us first consider the case in which L contains a modal operator and allows for indirect discourse. Thus L will contain such expressions as 'A says that B,' 'A believes that B,' 'It is necessary that if A believes that B, then A believes that C.' In this case we may establish that interchangeability is a sufficient condition for synonymity by the following considerations. Let us begin with a true assertion from arithmetic:

(1) $9 = 9$.

If we replace either occurrence of "9" in this sentence by any expression A such that 'A $= 9$' is true, then the result will again be true.

Next, consider the true sentence.

(2) $N(9 = 9)$.[8]

Here we may obtain a false result if we replace an occurrence of "9" by an occurrence of some other expression on the basis of a true identity sentence. Thus "N(the number of the planets $= 9$)" is false. However, if we replace an occurrence of "9" by any expression A such that 'A $= 9$' is logically true, then the result will again be true. Now, suppose that the following sentence is true:

(3) Jones believes that $9 = 9$.

In this case, replacing an occurrence of "9" by even a logically

8. I write 'Np' as an abbreviation for 'It is necessary that p.'

equivalent expression—for example, by "$3^2$"—may lead to false-hood. There is no guarantee that it *will* lead to falsehood, but we can see that even if in fact Jones happens to believe both that $9 = 9$ and that $9 = 3^2$, it is at least possible for him to believe one without believing the other.[9] In other words, the true sentence:

(4) N(Jones believes that $9 = 9$ if and only if Jones believes that $9 = 9$),

will become false if the last occurrence of "9" is replaced by an occurrence of the logically equivalent expression "$3^2$." Thus logical equivalence of expressions is not sufficient to guarantee inter-changeability in a language of the type we are now considering.

That nothing short of synonymity will guarantee interchange-ability in a language of this type follows from the fact that the truth-value of a sentence 'Jones believes that A' depends not upon the truth-value of the constituent A but upon its meaning. If A is replaced by any other expression not having the same meaning, the truth-value of 'Jones believes that A' *may* be changed, which implies that the truth-value of 'N(Jones believes that A if and only if Jones believes that A)' *will* be changed. Consequently, if two sentences A and B are not synonymous, they will not be interchangeable in all sentences of our lan-guage. Similar considerations lead to the further conclusion that if any two sentence constituents $x$ and $y$ are not synonymous, then they will not be interchangeable in the true sentence,

(5) N(Jones believes that . . . $x$ . . . if and only if Jones be-lieves that . . . $x$ . . .).

On the basis of this we may assert that if two expressions can be interchanged in all sentences of L without altering truth-values,

9. This assertion may of course be doubted. If it is false, then the co-gency of my argument is destroyed; and I am aware that there is at least one interpretation of belief sentences such that it is false. Thus, suppose that "9" and "$3^2$" are both abbreviations for descriptive phrases and have what Russell calls "primary occurrences" in the sentences "Jones believes that $9 = 9$" and "Jones believes that $9 = 3^2$." Then the two sentences just mentioned are logically equivalent. Nevertheless, I think that in the usual sense of "belief" the two sentences are logically independent; I therefore reject the proposed interpretation as paradoxical.

then they are synonymous. Hence, the proposed condition holds for languages containing modal operators and indirect discourse.

However, when the condition is applied to extensional languages, or to languages which are extensional except for the presence of modal operators, the results obtained are paradoxical. In languages of this sort all equivalent (or, respectively, logically equivalent) expressions would be synonymous, a result which is in violent conflict with ordinary usage of the term "synonymous." It seems to me that the reason for this conflict is simple; in its ordinary usage, the term "synonymous" is applied to the ordinary language, or at least to languages which are such as to permit modal sentences and indirect discourse. Thus, if we consider the question whether "2" and "4/2" are synonymous, we shall probably regard the language of arithmetic as a part of the ordinary language and decide the question in the negative, which would be in complete agreement with our criterion.

On the other hand, there are good reasons for making synonymity relative to the language in which the terms occurs. Suppose that we have a language L and we wish to say something in L which will establish that two expressions in L are not synonymous. The only way to do this is to find some true sentence in L which would not be true if the terms were synonymous. For example, "2" and "4/2" could be shown nonsynonymous by the true sentence, "Someone might believe that $1 + 1 = 2$ without believing that $1 + 1 = 4/2$." Now, given any pair of equivalent expressions in an extensional language $L_1$, it will be impossible to find in $L_1$ any true sentence indicating that the expressions are not synonymous; hence, for all that can be said in an extensional language, any two equivalent expressions are synonymous. Likewise, given any pair of logically equivalent expressions in a modal language $L_2$, it will not be possible to find a true sentence in $L_2$ that would be false if the expressions were not synonymous. Therefore, logically equivalent expressions will be synonymous, for all that can be said in $L_2$ to the contrary.[10] In

10. But, of course, for any two terms which are not logically equivalent it will be possible in the modal language to find a true sentence which would not be true if they were synonymous. For example, though "morning star" and "evening star" are equivalent, the negation of "N(morning star = evening star)" is a true sentence which indicates that these terms are not synonymous.

general, it seems natural to regard two expressions as synonymous in a language if there is no way in the language of distinguishing between their meanings. Thus it is natural to regard synonymity of terms as relative to the language in which the terms occur.

I shall conclude my discussion of the proposed condition of adequacy by offering some comments on other people's views.

Quine has discussed problems very closely related to those at hand, and no one can fail to be instructed by what he says.[11] However, it seems to me that his choice of terminology may lead one to suppose that what is essentially a question of synonymity is instead a question of designation. The following specific example (his own) will be of use in clarifying the point. Consider the sentences:

(6) Philip believes that Tegucigalpa is in Nicaragua.

(7) Tegucigalpa is the capital of Honduras.

Substitution into (6) on the basis of (7) gives

(8) Philip believes that the capital of Honduras is in Nicaragua.

Now apparently (6) and (8) are not logically equivalent. Quine seeks to explain this by asserting that the occurrence of "Tegucigalpa" in (6) is not "purely designative" and by claiming that only purely designative occurrences of names are subject to substitutivity on the basis of a true identity sentence. But this explanation is not a good one, as will appear from the following parallel case:

(9) Philip believes that $2^{10} < 1000$.

(10) $2^{10} = 1024$.

(11) Philip believes that $1024 < 1000$.

If we grant that (9) and (11) need not be equivalent, it is evident that the expression "$2^{10}$," like "Tegucigalpa," is subject to substitutivity in some contexts and not in others. Hence, in order

11. See "Notes on Existence and Necessity," *Journal of Philosophy,* 40 (1943): 113–127.

to apply Quine's mode of explanation here we shall have to say that some occurrences of "$2^{10}$" are purely designative and some are not. This, unfortunately, commits us to a kind of Platonism which no one is more anxious than Quine to avoid. He apparently wishes to assert that expressions like "$2^{10}$" *never* occur designatively, for he is of the opinion that there are no such things as numbers. Now if they never occur designatively, substitution on the basis of a true identity sentence will never be possible. But we know that it is possible. Hence, this sort of explanation is difficult to combine with nominalism. I should make it clear, however, that I do not object to Quine's view because it clashes with nominalism; my objection is rather that this particular problem may be treated independently of the nominalism-realism dispute. The sentences (6)–(8) and (9)–(11) show us that substitution on the basis of a true identity sentence cannot be made in a context governed by "believes that." We can discover and utilize this fact without ever taking up the question whether number expressions or any other expressions designate anything.

C. I. Lewis has explicated synonymity in such a way that synthetic sentences are synonymous if and only if they are logically equivalent.[12] It is easy to see that this is not in agreement with our criterion. For example, consider the sentences:

(12) Jones believes that he has one nose.

(13) Jones believes that the number of his noses is equal to–$(e\pi^4)$.

It will probably be generally agreed that these sentences might well have opposite truth-values; if this is possible, then the synthetic subsentences, though they are logically equivalent, are not synonymous according to our criterion. The example chosen need not have been so extreme. In the physical sciences there are many pairs of synthetic sentences which are logically equivalent to each other but which, unfortunately, are not interchangeable in belief contexts, as any teacher will confirm.

12. See "The Modes of Meaning," *Philosophy and Phenomenological Research*, 4 (1943–1944): 236–250; and *An Analysis of Knowledge and Valuation* (La Salle, Ill., Open Court, 1946), p. 86.

Arne Naess in connection with some very important empirical research he is doing on the subject of synonymity, has mentioned several possible definitions of the term.[13] Some of these do not satisfy our criterion. According to one, for example, two sentences would be synonymous if and only if the same states of affairs would confirm or disconfirm the propositions which they express. According to this, it seems to me, all logically equivalent sentences would be synonymous; but we have seen that logical equivalence is not a strong enough condition for interchangeability in a language containing indirect discourse. According to another possibility mentioned by Naess, two sentences are synonymous if every sentence derivable from one is derivable from the other, and conversely. Now the exact meaning of this depends upon how the word "derivable" is interpreted, but if logically equivalent sentences are derivable from one another, then logically equivalent sentences would be synonymous under this definition, too. Consequently, both of these possibilities for defining "synonymity" would have to be rejected as inadequate, if our criterion of adequacy were accepted.

Carnap has proposed the concept of intensional isomorphism as an appropriate explicatum for synonymity.[14] It seems to me that this is the best proposal that has been made by anyone to date. However, it has, along with its merits, some rather odd consequences. For instance, let "D" and "D'" be abbreviations for two intensionally isomorphic sentences. Then the following sentences are also intensionally isomorphic:

(14) Whoever believes that D, believes that D.

(15) Whoever believes that D, believes that D'.

But nobody doubts that whoever believes that D believes that D. Therefore, nobody doubts that whoever believes that D believes that D'. This seems to suggest that, for any pair of intensionally isomorphic sentences—let them be abbreviated by "D" and "D'"—if anybody even doubts that whoever believes that D believes that D', then Carnap's explication is incorrect. What is more, *any*

13. See *Interpretation and Preciseness*, I: *Survey of Basic Concepts* (mim., Oslo, 1947).

14. See *Meaning and Necessity* (Univ. of Chicago Press, 1947), pp. 56 ff.

adequate explication of synonymity will have this result, for the validity of the argument is not affected if we replace the words "intensionally isomorphic" by the word "synonymous" throughout.

## III

Interpretation is a matter of prime importance to philosophers in at least two respects. In the first place, every philosopher who deserves the name wants to understand the writings of his fellows and predecessors, and this often requires the utmost in careful and skilled interpretation. Secondly, many of the problems which philosophers seek to solve are themselves problems of interpretation or else correspond to such problems in certain characteristic ways. Both of these respects will be discussed in the present section.

Philosophical writing seems to me to have a pair of characteristics which are especially significant in the present connection. One is that it is argumentative. Very little of what would be regarded as genuine philosophical writing consists of mere musings. On the contrary, philosophers (*qua* philosophers) are nearly always trying to argue in behalf of some thesis. Often the arguments are dfficult to follow; often, when they can be understood, they are seen to be invalid. Nevertheless, it seems correct to say that philosophical writing is largely argumentative.

The other characteristic to which I wish to draw attention (and to which I fear I am drawing attention) is that of relative unclarity. Whether the fault be with the subject matter or with the philosophers or with both, we must grant that the products are often the very reverse of lucid. I do not mention this in order to derogate from the value of philosophical writing, nor on the other hand do I bring it up in order to suggest that philosophers are persons who think deeply and whose communications are consequently not easy to understand; I only mention the relative opaqueness of philosophical writing as a matter of fact.

As a result of these factors we often become aware, in reading the discourse of some philosopher, that he is presenting an argument in behalf of some thesis, but at the same time we are unable to understand either the thesis or the argument well enough to decide questions of truth and validity. Thus arises the need for an interpretation. We require a translation of the obscure discourse into a body of discourse which is probably much longer than the original but which consists of expressions more readily intelligible to us than the original expressions were. After the interpretation has been constructed we are better able to decide upon the truth and validity of the original discourse. Then we are at least able to make comments of the following form: 'If by A he means B, then what he says is true (or false), or his argument is valid (or invalid).' In my opinion this is the form in which philosophical criticism ought always to be made, but usually, of course, the hypothesis 'If by A he means B' is omitted.

In this procedure the chances of failing to do justice to the author under examination are very great, and the greatest danger lies in assuming that the interpretation which is the basis of the criticism is a good one. It will be instructive to examine some particular instances of philosophical criticism, with a view toward seeing in detail how errors of interpretation can lead to injustice in criticism. The first case to be presented is artificial and much simplified; yet it will be serious enough, no doubt, to provoke comment.

Suppose that in the writings of some philosopher we find this strange argument:

(1) Socrates is human.
(2) Human is human.
(3) For every A, B, C: if A is C and B is C, then A resembles B with respect to being C.
(4) Therefore, Socrates resembles human with respect to being human.[15]

In behalf of the premises of his argument, the author might offer some such considerations as the following. That Socrates is human is asserted as a matter of fact. The statement "Human is human" is an instance of "A is A," and hence is not only true but is necessarily true. The third premise is to be regarded as analytic be-

15. I do not propose this argument as a model of English composition, but rather as an example of discourse for which an interpretation is needed.

cause of the meaning of "resembles," but it may at least be illustrated by examples. So, if Socrates is a philosopher and Plato is
a philosopher, then Socrates resembles Plato (with respect to
being a philosopher); likewise, if lead is heavy and gold is
heavy, then lead resembles gold (with respect to being heavy).
Also, if Mark Twain is the author of *Innocents Abroad* and Samuel Clemens is the author of *Innocents Abroad*, then Mark Twain
resembles Samuel Clemens[16] with respect to authoring this book.

Given these considerations in behalf of the truth of the premises, and given the obvious fact that the argument is valid in
form, we are apparently forced to accept the conclusion, which
seems to express the Platonic view that Socrates resembles the
Idea of Human, that is, that he resembles humanity itself. But
there are certain obvious objections to the argument; and let us
consider these. (I shall ignore the syntactical strangeness of the
conclusion and of the second premise, since this seems to be due
to a purely accidental feature of the English language, namely,
that there are two terms, "humanity" and "human," which express the same property but which are such that syntax forbids
their interchange.)

Probably the most serious objection that would be raised could
be stated as follows. The word "is," as it appears in this argument, is ambiguous. Sometimes it means the same as the phrase
"has the property," and thus when the philosopher says "Socrates
is human" he means that Socrates has the property Human. But
sometimes "is" means the same as "is identical with," so that the
sentence "Human is human" means that the property Human is
identical with the property Human. Now the third premise is
plausible only so long as the word "is" retains the same meaning
at both of its occurrences in the statement. Thus, the argument
is either invalid or one of its premises is false.

16. This last is obviously an extreme case, in which the resemblance is
very close! But the mere fact that we would ordinarily make the stronger
statement, that Mark Twain *is* Samuel Clemens, should not lead us to
suppose that the weaker statement, that Mark Twain *resembles* Samuel
Clemens, is either false or meaningless. Thus, if I see someone on the street
and say to my companion, "Whoever that is, he certainly resembles President Truman," my assertion will not be false or nonsensical if it turns out
that the man actually is President Truman.

Let us examine this objection more closely. It rests upon an interpretation of the original argument, that is, upon a translation of its four sentences into the following four sentences:

(1) Socrates has the property Human.

(2) The property Human is identical with the property Human.

(3) For every A, B, C: if A has the property C and B has the property C, then A resembles B with respect to having the property C.

(4) Therefore, Socrates resembles the property Human with respect to having the property Human.

But the argument, as thus interpreted, involves a clear *non sequitur,* and this fact is supposed to show that the original argument is really defective even though it appears to be a valid argument with true premises.

In a similar way, other interpretations of the same argument lead to the conclusion that it is unacceptable, either because it is invalid or because at least one of its premises is false. For instance, if we resolutely translate 'A is B' everywhere into 'A has the property B,' we get the following interpretation:

(1) Socrates has the property Human.

(2) Human has the property Human.

(3) For every A, B, C: if A has the property C and B has the property C, then A resembles B with respect to having the property C.

(4) Therefore, Socrates resembles Human with respect to having the property Human.

In this interpretation the argument is valid and the first and third premises seem acceptable enough, but serious difficulties stand in the way of our assenting to the second premise. As Russell says in criticizing Plato: "I can say 'Socrates is human,' 'Plato is human,' and so on. In all these statements, it may be assumed that the word 'human' has exactly the same meaning. But whatever it means, it means something which is not of the same kind as Socrates, Plato, and the rest of the individuals who compose the human race. 'Human' is an adjective; it would be nonsense to say 'human is human.' " [17] Here Russell is evidently thinking of "Human is human" as meaning that the property Human has the property Human, and not as an instance of the theorem "$\varphi\, z = \varphi\, z$."

If, then, we agree to the first interpretation of the argument, we shall say that the author has committed the fallacy of using the same term in different senses at certain crucial places in the argument, thus rendering the argument invalid; and if we agree to the second interpretation, we may say that the author "has no understanding of philosophical syntax," and that the second premise is false or meaningless. Thus, under either interpretation, we shall deny that the conclusion is established as true by this argument.

Now, in my opinion, the dangers in such a critical procedure are quite evident but usually ignored. In the case at hand, none of the considerations advanced are sufficient to justify condemnation of the argument. For in spite of the fact that there are two interpretations of "is" such that the argument is not conclusive under either of these interpretations, it remains to be shown that no plausible interpretation can be found in which the premises are true and the argument valid. This last would not be an easy thing to do, and it is probable that very few critics would wish to postpone criticism of a piece of philosophical writing until it had been ascertained that there was no plausible interpretation under which that piece of writing would be acceptable. Usually the procedure of critics is quite the reverse; each thinks that he knows well enough how the English language is used—that is, each acts as though *his* interpretation or interpretations were the only ones possible—and consequently if the passage under scrutiny doesn't make sense when interpreted in his particular way, he judges that it doesn't make sense at all.

Hence, to return to the argument which we are using as an example, we must consider the possibility that neither of the two interpretations proposed is faithful to the sense of the original text. This amounts to considering the possibility that besides the predicative sense of the word "is," in which it always expresses a

17. *A History of Western Philosophy* (New York, Simon & Schuster, 1945), p. 127.

relation between things of different type, and the identity sense of the word, in which it always expresses a relation between things of the same type, there may be another more general sense of "is" such that the argument is valid when the occcurrences of "is" are understood in this sense. "Well!" the objectors will immediately reply, "if there is such a sense, what is it?"

Before attempting to answer this question, let us try to decide what kind of answer is wanted. Probably no one expects the word "is" to be defined ostensively. This being so, we may fairly take the question to be a request for an English expression that is synonymous with "is." The objectors have suggested that the phrase "has the property" is synonymous with "is" in some of its occurrences, and that the phrase "is identical with" is synonymous with it in its other occurrences, and now they expect us either to accept their interpretations as final or else to set forth a phrase which is clearly meaningful and which can be regarded as synonymous with "is" in all or nearly all of its occurrences. But we may observe at once that the possibility of doing this depends in part upon the richness of English. It depends upon whether the English language happens to contain an expression which is synonymous with "is." Whether or not it does so is a purely contingent matter. If it should be the case that it does not, this would not suffice to show that there is no single sense which the word possesses in all its occurrences. As many writers have pointed out, there are in general strong reasons against the existence of synonymous expression in a conversational language. Usually we simply do not need two expressions with the same meaning, and if there are any synonyms at all, this may be ascribed more to the ancestry of the language than to its utility. Consequently, anyone who asks what the sense of a linguistic expression is ought to be aware that there is no good reason for supposing the question answerable. If he does succeed in getting a satisfactory definition, he may thank fortune; if he does not, his only recourse is to discover the meaning of the expression from observing how it is used.

Let us now attempt to find an interpretation such that under this interpretation the argument in question is translated into a valid argument with true premises. We may proceed as follows.

Generic terms like "Human" are commonly regarded as having classes for their extensions and properties for their intensions. Suppose that proper names, for example "Socrates," were also regarded in this way; then the extension of "Socrates" would be the unit class of Socrates and the intension would be the defining characteristic of Socrates. This supposition, no doubt, would represent the height of Platonism. Individuals would turn out to be abstract entities, and thus we would have to imagine it possible for us not only to see an abstract entity but even to be one! But whether or not this interpretation is Platonistic is irrelevant to the present discussion (though I shall here express my confidence that if every individual suddenly turned into his unit class, no one would notice the difference). The problem at hand is merely to construct an interpretation. Accordingly, supposing that we understand proper names as indicated, let us interpret "is" by the phrase "is included in." The argument then becomes:

(1) Socrates is included in Human.
(2) Human is included in Human.
(3) For every A, B, C: if A is included in C and B is included in C, then A resembles B with respect to being included in C.
(4) Therefore, Socrates resembles Human with respect to being included in Human.

The premises are true, since both the unit class of Socrates and the class Human are included in the class Human, and since it is not implausible to interpret "resembles" in such a way that (3) holds. Further, the argument is of valid form; therefore, we may say that under the interpretation offered, the argument is a valid argument with true premises.

I hope that the point of this fantastic example is clear. The original argument contained "Socrates is human" as its first premise. We must not suppose that the author necessarily meant what we would express by the sentence "the individual Socrates had the property Human." He may have meant what we would express by "the unit class of Socrates is included in the class Human" or "the defining property of Socrates is included in the property Human." It seems to me, therefore, that if an author's arguments become invalid under a given interpretation, common sense requires that not only the capability of the author but also the correctness of the interpretation come under suspicion.

For a second and less artificial example of philosophical argument based on questionable interpretation, I shall turn again to some aspects of the nominalism of Quine. According to Quine, it is possible to determine that a man is a "platonist" by examining how he uses variables of quantification. The term "platonist" in this sense refers to anyone who supposes that universals exist. Quine's criterion seems to be as follows: whoever applies quantifiers to object variables presupposes that there are such entities as objects; whoever applies quantifiers to class variables presupposes that there are such entities as classes; etc.[18] In behalf of this method of ascertaining ontological commitments, Quine says:

> The quantifier '$(Ex)$' means 'there is an entity $x$ such that,' and the quantifier '$(x)$' means 'every entity $x$ is such that.' The bound variables of a theory range over all the entities of which the theory treats. That classical mathematics treats of universals, or affirms that there are universals, means simply that classical mathematics requires universals as values of its bound variables. When we say, e.g., that
>
> $$(Ex) \ (x \text{ is prime and } 5 < x < 11)$$
>
> we are saying that *there is* something which is prime and between 5 and 11; and this entity is in fact the number 7, a universal, if such there be.[19]

It seems quite clear, therefore, that Quine's view rests upon the assumption that sentences beginning with the existential quantifier "$(Ex)$" are to be interpreted by sentences beginning with the phrase "there is an entity $x$ such that." As far as I can see, this assumption is without justification. In the first place,

---

18. Provided, of course, that the quantifiers are part of the primitive notation of the language. See Quine, "Designation and Existence," *Journal of Philosophy*, 36 (1939): 701–709; "On Universals," *Journal of Symbolic Logic*, 12 (1947): 74–84; and the article cited in note 11 above.

19. Quine, "On Universals," p. 75.

if we examine the actual usage of mathematicians and logicians, we find that the existential quantifier is read in many different ways: "there exists an $x$ such that," "for some $x$," "for some values of '$x$,' " etc. These various phrases may or may not be intended by their users as always introducing ontological assertions. But in the second place, it is possible to interpret existential quantifiers in such a way that no ontological commitments are involved, save possibly commitments to the existence of expressions in the language. For instance, the sentence "$(Ex)$ ($x$ is prime and $5 < x < 11$)" may be interpreted by the sentence "there is a constant such that the sentence which results from substituting this constant for '$x$' in the matrix '$x$ is prime and $5 < x < 11$' is true." Thus one might well use the existential quantifier on number variables without committing himself to the view that there are such things as numbers. This method of interpreting existential quantifiers is well known, and, to be sure, it involves certain difficulties. For example, if there is something for which there is no constant in the object language, then it is possible for "$(Ex)$ ($x$ is mortal)" to be false even if something is moral. But these difficulties can be remedied to a great extent; anyhow, the interpretation is not so patently untenable that some other interpretation can be accepted as self-evidently correct. The point here, as in the other example, is that it is philosophically dangerous to assume that a given interpretation is the correct one.

This completes what I have to say concerning the interpretation of philosophical writing. The other topic of the present section is the relation between certain problems of philosophy and problems of interpretation. I shall begin by giving two examples of how philosophical problems may be expressed as problems of interpretation.

The thesis of phenomenalism might be stated roughly as follows: for every sentence about material things there exists another sentence which is about sense contents and which is synonymous with it. Possibly a better formulation of the thesis could be obtained if we specified, by lists or otherwise, two sets of terms, to be called "material-object terms" and "sense-data terms," respectively. Then we could restate the thesis in the following way: for every sentence containing a material-object term there is a synonymous sentence which contains only sense-data terms together with certain logical constants. In a corresponding way, the naturalistic position in ethics might be expressed by the statement: for every sentence containing an ethical term there is a synonymous sentence containing only terms of the approved, naturalistic variety. Again, we would have somehow to specify the set of ethical terms and the set of naturalistic terms, perhaps by lists. Presumably the terms "good," "bad," "right," "wrong," and the like, would be on the ethical list, and the naturalistic list would contain such words as "pleasure," "approval," "utility," "happiness," and the like.

Now it is important to be very clear about what does and what does not follow from the fact that these positions may be stated in the way described. For instance, does it follow that phenomenalism and naturalism are "purely verbal" theses? It certainly does not. For to find an adequate method of translating sentences containing the word "good" is no more and no less difficult than to find a so-called real definition of good, and to decide whether there is an adequate method of translating material-object sentences into sense-data sentences is exactly as difficult as to solve the metaphysical problem of whether phenomenalism is true. Again, the procedure used by Socrates in his attempt to discover a real definition of piety is essentially the same procedure that one would have to use in order to discover a complex expression synonymous with the word "piety." In general, it seems to me, we do not get rid of philosophical problems by representing them as problems of translation or interpretation; the situation is rather that the solution of either version of the problem always involves the solution of the other version.

This raises the following question: if a linguistic problem corresponding to a given philosophical problem cannot be solved unless the latter is solved, what is the use of giving attention to the linguistic version? The answer is that the linguistic version often serves to clarify the nature of the problem and to show, unfortunately, that the original problem was even more complicated than had been supposed. Consider, for example, the following linguistic version of the thesis usually called "hedonism":

for every sentence containing the term "good" there is a synonymous sentence which does not contain "good" or any other ethical term, but which does contain the term "pleasure." If we investigate the problem by means of this formulation we are led
to make certain distinctions which are, in my opinion, very important. We see at once that the decision whether a certain type
of hedonism is true will involve deciding whether certain sentences are synonymous. Since synonymity is relative to a language, we shall need to specify some language, or, what comes
to the same thing, we shall need to specify what *degree* of synonymity is required.[20] Thus, suppose that we are interested in the
synonymity or lack of synonymity of the expressions "good" and
"productive of pleasure." If we deal only with extensional contexts, then we can establish that these terms are synonymous if
we can establish that whatever is good is productive of pleasure
and whatever is productive of pleasure is good. If we speak with
reference to a language which is extensional except for the presence of the modal operator "it is necessary that . . . ," then to
show that the two terms are synonymous we shall have to establish not only that all good things are pleasant, and conversely,
but also that it is impossible for something to be good without
being pleasant, or to be pleasant without being good. If, as is
more likely, we speak with reference to a language containing
indirect discourse, then even though the predicators "good" and
"productive of pleasure" were logically equivalent, they might
not be synonymous. Thus, when the problem of whether or not
this form of hedonism is true is stated as a problem of interpretation, it becomes clear that there are at least three distinguishable problems masquerading as one. It is important to be aware
of this, since when we examine the writings of ethicists on hedonism, we find that those who support it usually try to show
that the expressions are synonymous in the first sense (i.e., that
"good" and "productive of pleasure" apply to the same things),

20. I say that two terms are synonymous to a low degree in the natural
language if they are synonymous in the largest extensional sublanguage of
the natural language; they are synonymous to a higher degree if they are
synonymous in the largest sublanguage which is extensional except for containing modal operators; and they are synonymous to the highest degree if
they are synonymous in the natural language taken as a whole.

while those who attack it try to show that the expressions are not synonymous in the second or third senses (i.e., that it is possible for something to be good and not pleasant, or that we may believe something to be good without believing it pleasant). Thus these opponents hold positions which are perfectly compatible—if, I hasten to add, I have interpreted them correctly.

In this way, the linguistic version of a philosophical problem may be a useful heuristic device for attacking the problem, just as in deciding certain questions of geography it is useful to translate them into questions regarding the positions of marks on a map. But just as it would be ludicrous to suppose that maps constitute the entire subject matter of geography, so also it would be a great mistake to suppose that philosophy is or ought to be nothing more than the study of language. I trust that what I have said here has served to illustrate, if not to establish, the truth of that conclusion.

# THE MEANING OF A WORD

## J. L. Austin

*The middle section of J. L. Austin's "The Meaning of a Word" contains a sketchy criticism of the analytic-synthetic distinction which actually was written long before the reprinted pieces by Quine and White but which was not published until 1961. Austin attacks the attempt to retain the dichotomy in ordinary language. Given any judgment, 'x is y,' Austin points out that it seems only common sense to say about it, "x is either part of the meaning of y or it is not," but common sense misleads us in this case. Austin has argued earlier that meanings are not the sort of things which have parts and that one really cannot make sense of the phrase "the meaning of a word"; this argument is contained in the first section of the article which is not included here.*

From *Philosophical Papers*, ed. J. O. Urmson and G. J. Warnock. Reprinted by permission of The Clarendon Press.

Austin's main argument is twofold: the features of ordinary languages and the occurrence of extraordinary situations preclude retaining the strict dichotomy between analytic and synthetic judgments. The way in which the distinction between syntactics and semantics actually operates in ordinary languages raises a problem because, according to Austin, ordinary languages contain no (or very few) explicit rules or conventions, "no rigid separation of what is syntactical and what is semantical." Austin uses the well-known example, "The cat is on the mat, and I do not believe it" to illustrate this point. This claim seems absurd. The two conjuncts seem incompatible. If the often-used convention 'either *p* is compatible with not-*r* or *p* implies *r*' is applied, then most of us would be tempted to say "'The cat is on the mat' implies 'I believe it'" if our choice is limited by this convention to this implication or to the compatibility of 'The cat is on the mat' with 'I do not believe it.' "The cat is on the mat, and I do not believe it" is not self-contradictory. It does not violate some explicit syntactical convention. Likewise, "'The cat is on the mat' implies 'I believe it'" does not follow from some explicit convention; if the speaker is deliberately lying when he says "The cat is on the mat," it would seem to be absurd to insist that he believes it. The apparent infelicity about uttering, "The cat is on the mat, and I do not believe it" arises, Austin says, because of implicit semantical conventions concerning the ways in which words are used in particular situations. Careful analysis of the richness and complexity of such situations "should cure us once and for all of this bogy," Austin says, "of insisting on classifying sentences as either *analytic* or *synthetic*."

Extraordinary situations (Quine's recalcitrant experiences?) also are an indication of why the analytic-synthetic distinction does not hold in ordinary language. "Ordinary language breaks down in extraordinary cases," Austin says, and "words fail us." Thinking of such cases might be difficult, Austin tells us, because the imagination is "blinkered" by language, but such cases do occur. Austin's example of such a case is saying about a man, "Either he is at home or he is not at home," just after the man has died; in such a situation, Austin says, neither would be correct.

*There are many situations which may and actually do develop which would, in Austin's words, "need new and better language," and such situations force an abandonment of the strict dichotomy between analytic and synthetic statements.*

*The most significant question which immediately arises is whether Austin has really raised substantive problems with the analytic-synthetic distinction or whether he is simply pointing to a third class of gray statements which do not seem to fit appropriately into either category—a point made or conceded by nearly everyone.*

Constantly we ask the question, 'Is *y* the meaning, or *part* of the meaning, or *contained* in the meaning, of *x*?—or is it *not*?' A favorite way of putting the question is to ask, 'Is the judgment "*x* is *y*" analytic or synthetic?' Clearly, we suppose, *y must* be *either* a part of the meaning of *x*, *or* not any part of it. And, if *y* is a part of the meaning of *x*, to say '*x* is *y*' will be self-contradictory: while if it is *not* a part of the meaning of *x*, to say '*x* is not *y*' will present no difficulty—such a state of affairs will be readily 'conceivable.' This seems to be the merest common sense. And no doubt it *would* be the merest common sense if 'meanings' were things in some ordinary sense which contained parts in some ordinary sense. But they are *not*. Unfortunately, many philosophers who know they are not, still speak as though *y* must either be or not be 'part of the meaning' of *x*. But this is the point: *if* 'explaining the meaning of a word' is really the complicated sort of affair that we have seen it to be, and *if* there is really nothing to call 'the meaning of a word'—*then* phrases like 'part of the meaning of the word *x*' are completely undefined; it is left hanging in the air, we do not know what it means at all. *We are using a working-model which fails to fit the facts that we really wish to talk about.* When we consider what we really do want to talk about, and not the working-model, what would really be meant at all by a judgment being 'analytic or synthetic'? We simply do not know. Of course, we feel inclined to say, 'I can easily produce examples of analytic and synthetic judgments; for instance, I should confidently say

"Being a professor is *not* part of the meaning of being a man" and so forth.' 'A is A is analytic.' Yes, but it is when we are required to give a *general definition* of what we mean by 'analytic' or 'synthetic,' and when we are required to justify our dogma that *every* judgment is either analytic or synthetic, that we find we have, in fact, nothing to fall back upon *except our working-model.* From the start, it is clear that our working-model fails to do justice, for example, to the distinction between syntactics and semantics: for instance, talking about the contradictory of every sentence having to be either self-contradictory or not so, is to talk as though all sentences which we are prohibited from saying were sentences which offended against *syntactical* rules, and could be formally reduced to verbal self-contradictions. But this overlooks all semantical considerations, which philosophers are sadly prone to do. Let us consider two cases of some things which we simply *cannot say:* although they are *not* 'self-contradictory' and although—and this of course is where many will have axes to grind—we cannot possibly be tempted to say that we have 'synthetic *a priori*' knowledge of their contradictions.

Let us begin with a case which, being about *sentences* rather than *words,* is not quite in point, but which may encourage us. Take the well-known sentence 'The cat is on the mat, and I do not believe it.' That seems absurd. On the other hand 'The cat is on the mat, and I believe it' seems trivial. If we were to adopt a customary dichotomy, and to say *either* a proposition *p* implies another proposition *r, or p* is perfectly compatible with not-*r*, we should at once in our present case be tempted to say that 'The cat is on the mat' *implies* 'I believe it': hence both the triviality of adding 'and I believe it' and the absurdity of adding 'and I do not believe it.' But of course 'the cat is on the mat' does *not* imply 'Austin believes the cat is on the mat': nor even 'the speaker believes the cat is on the mat'—for the speaker may be lying. The doctrine which is produced in this case is, that not *p* indeed, but *asserting p* implies 'I (who assert *p*) believe *p*.' And here 'implies' must be given a special sense: for of course it is not that 'I assert *p*' implies (in the ordinary sense)

'I believe *p*,' for I may be lying. It is the sort of sense in which by asking a question I 'imply' that I do not know the answer to it. By asserting *p* I *give it to be understood* that I believe *p*.

Now the reason why I cannot say 'The cat is on the mat and I do not believe it' is not that it offends against syntactics in the sense of being in some way 'self-contradictory.' What prevents my saying it, is rather some semantic convention (implicit, of course), about the way we use words *in situations.* What precisely is the account to be given in this case we need not ask. Let us rather notice one significant feature of it. Whereas '*p* and I believe it' is somehow trivial, and '*p* and I do not believe it' is somehow nonsense, a third sentence '*p* and *I might not have* believed it' makes perfectly good sense. Let us call these three sentences Q, not-Q, and 'might not Q.' Now what prohibits us from saying '*p*' implies 'I believe *p*' in the ordinary sense of 'implies,' is precisely shown by this fact: that although not-Q is (*somehow*) absurd, 'might not Q' is not at all absurd. For in ordinary cases of implication, not merely is not-Q absurd, but 'might not Q' is *also* absurd: for example, 'triangles are figures and triangles have no shape' is no more absurd than 'triangles are figures and triangles might have had no shape.' Consideration of the sentence 'might not Q' will afford a rough test as to whether *p* 'implies' *r* in the *ordinary* sense, or in the special sense, of 'implies.'

Bearing this in mind, let us now consider a sentence which, as I claim, cannot possibly be classified as *either* 'analytic' *or* 'synthetic.' I refer to the sentence, 'This *x* exists,' where *x* is a sensum, for example, 'This noise exists.' In endeavoring to classify it, one party would point to the triviliality of 'This noise exists,' and to the absurdity of 'This noise does not exist.' They would say, therefore, that *existence* is 'part of the meaning of' *this.* But another party would point out, that 'This noise might not have existed' makes perfectly good sense. *They* would say, therefore, that *existence* cannot be 'part of the meaning of' *this.*

Both parties, as we are now in a position to see, would be correct in their *arguments,* but incorrect in their *conclusions.* What seems to be true is that *using the word 'this'* (not: the word 'this') *gives it to be understood that the* sensum referred to 'exists.'

Perhaps, historically, this fact about the sentence-trio, 'This noise exists,' 'This noise does not exist,' and 'This noise might not have existed,' was pointed out before any philosopher had had time to pronounce that 'This noise exists' is analytic, or is synthetic. But such a pronouncement might well have been made: and *to this day,* even when the fact has been pointed out, many philosophers *worry* about the case, supposing the sentence *must* be one or the other but painfully aware of the difficulties in choosing either. I wish to point out that consideration of the analogy between this case and the other, should cure us once and for all of this bogy, and of insisting on classifying sentences as *either* analytic *or* synthetic. It may encourage us to consider again what the facts in their actual complexity really are. (One thing it suggests is a reconsideration of 'Caesar is bald' and similar propositions: but I cannot go into that.)

So far, however, we have scarcely begun in earnest: we have merely felt that initial trepidation, experienced when the firm ground of prejudice begins to slip away beneath the feet. Perhaps there are other cases, or other sorts of cases, where it will not be possible to say either that *y* is a 'part of the meaning' of *x* or that it is not, without being misleading.

Suppose we take the case of 'being thought good by me' and 'being approved of by me.' Are we to rush at this with the dichotomy: *either* 'being approved of by me' *is* part of the meaning of 'being thought good by me' *or* it is *not*? It is *obvious* that 'I think *x* good but I do not approve of it' is self-contradictory? Of course it is not *verbally* self-contradictory. That it either is or is not 'really' self-contradictory would seem to be difficult to establish. Of course, we think, it must be one or the other—only 'it's difficult to decide *which*': or 'it depends on how you use the words.' But are those really the difficulties which baffle us? Of course, *if* it were certain that every sentence *must* be either analytic or synthetic, those *must* be the difficulties. But then, it is not certain: no account even of what the distinction means, is given except by reference to our shabby

working-model. I suggest that 'I think *x* good but I do not approve of it' may very well be neither self-contradictory nor
yet 'perfectly good sense' in the way in which 'I think *x* exciting
but I do not approve of it' *is* 'perfectly good sense.'

Perhaps this example does not strike you as awkward. It
cannot be expected that all examples will appeal equally to all
hearers. Let us take some others. Is 'What is good ought to
exist' anaytic or synthetic? According to Moore's theory, this
must be 'synthetic': yet he constantly in *Principia Ethica* takes
its truth for granted. And that illustrates one of the main drawbacks of insisting on saying that a sentence *must* be either analytic or synthetic: you are almost certain to have left on your
hands some general sentences which are certainly not analytic
but which you find it difficult to conceive being false: that is,
you are landed with 'synthetic *a priori* knowledge.' Take that
sentence of ill fame 'Pink is more like red than black.' It is rash
to pronounce this 'synthetic *a priori* knowledge' on the ground
that 'being more like red than black' is not 'part of the meaning'
or 'part of the definition' of 'pink' and that it is not 'conceivable' that pink should be more like black than red: I dare say,
so far as those phrases have any clear meaning, that it *is not*:
but the question is: *is* the thing therefore 'synthetic' *a priori*
knowledge?

Or, again, take some examples from Berkeley: is *extended* 'part
of the meaning' of *colored* or of *shaped,* or *shaped* 'part of the
meaning' of *extended*? Is 'est sed non percipitur' self-contradictory (when said of a sensum), or is it not? When we worry
thus, is it not worth considering the possibility that we are
oversimplifying?

What we are to say in these cases, what even the possibilities
are, I do not at present clearly see. (1) Evidently, we must
throw away the old working-model as soon as we take account
even of the existence of a distinction between syntactics and
semantics. (2) But evidently also, our *new* working-model, the
supposed 'ideal' language, is in many ways a most inadequate
model of any *actual* language: its careful separation of syntactics from semantics, its lists of explicitly formulated rules and
conventions, and its careful delimitation of their spheres of

operation—all are misleading. An *actual* language has few, if any, explicit conventions, no sharp limits to the spheres of operation of rules, no rigid separation of what is syntactical and what semantical. (3) Finally, I think I can see that there are difficulties about our powers of imagination, and about the curious way in which it is enslaved by words.

To encourage ourselves in the belief that this sort of consideration may play havoc with the distinction 'analytic or synthetic,' let us consider a similar and more familiar case. It seems, does it not, perfectly obvious that every proposition must have a contradictory? Yet it does not turn out so. Suppose that I live in harmony and friendship for four years with a cat: and then it delivers a philippic. We ask ourselves, perhaps, 'Is it a real cat? or is it *not* a real cat?' 'Either it *is*, or it *is not*, but we cannot be sure which.' Now actually, that is not so: *neither* 'It is a real cat' *nor* 'it is not a real cat' fits the facts semantically: each is designed for other situations than this one: you could not say the former of something which delivers philippics, nor yet the latter of something which has behaved as this has for four years. There are similar difficulties about choosing between 'This *is* a hallucination' and 'This is *not* a hallucination.' With sound instinct, the plain man turns in such cases to Watson and says 'Well now, *what would you* say?' 'How would you *describe* it?' The difficulty is just that: there is *no* short description which is not misleading: the only thing to do, and that can easily be done, is to set out the description of the facts at length. Ordinary language breaks down in extraordinary cases. (In such cases, the cause of the breakdown is semantical.) Now no doubt an *ideal* language would *not* break down, whatever happened. In doing physics, for example, where our language is tightened up in order precisely to describe complicated and unusual cases concisely, we *prepare linguistically for the worst*. In ordinary language we do not: *words fail us*. If we talk as though an ordinary must be like an ideal language, we shall misrepresent the facts.

Consider now 'being extended' and 'being shaped.' In ordinary life we never get into a situation where we learn to say that anything is extended but not shaped nor conversely. We have all learned to use, and have used, the words only in cases where it is correct to use both. Supposing now someone says '*x* is extended but has no shape.' Somehow we cannot see what this 'could mean'—there are no semantic conventions, explicit or implicit, to cover this case: yet it is not prohibited in any way—there are no limiting rules about what we might or might not say *in extraordinary cases*. It is not *merely* the difficulty of imagining or experiencing extraordinary cases, either, which causes worry. There is this too: we can only describe what it is we are trying to imagine, by means of words which precisely describe and evoke the *ordinary* case, which we are trying to think away. Ordinary language *blinkers* the already feeble imagination. It would be difficult, in this way, if I were to say 'Can I think of a case where a man would be neither at home nor not at home?' This is inhibiting, because I think of the *ordinary* case where I ask 'Is he at home?' and get the answer, 'No': when certainly he is not at home. But supposing I happen *first* to think of the situation when I call on him just after he has died: then I see at once it would be wrong to say either. So in our case, the only thing to do is to imagine or experience all kinds of odd situations, and then suddenly round on oneself and ask: there, *now* would I say that, being extended it must be shaped? A new idiom might in odd cases be demanded.

I should like to say, in concluding this section, that in the course of stressing that we must pay attention to the facts of *actual* language, what we can and cannot say, and *precisely* why, another and converse point takes shape. Although it will not do to force actual language to accord with some preconceived model: it *equally* will not do, having discovered the facts about 'ordinary usage' *to rest content* with that, as though there were nothing more to be discussed and discovered. There may be plenty that might happen and does happen which would need new and better language to describe it in. Very often philosophers are only engaged on this task, when they seem to be perversely using words in a way which makes no sense according to 'ordinary usage.' There may be extraordinary facts, even about our everyday experience, which plain men and plain language overlook.

# MEANING AND SYNONYMY

# IN NATURAL LANGUAGES

## Rudolf Carnap

*In "Meaning and Synonymy in Natural Languages" Carnap attempts to develop a procedure for determining the intensions of predicates. That such a procedure is possible is what Carnap calls "the intensionalist thesis," according to which the assignment of an intension is "an empirical hypothesis" which can be confirmed or falsified by observable "language behavior."*

*Generalizing this procedure, Carnap claims that we arrive at the procedure for determining the intension of any concept for any person, at any time, and in any natural language. "This general concept of intension may be characterized roughly as follows, leaving subtleties aside: the intension of a predicate Q for a speaker X is the general condition which an object y must fulfill in order for X to be willing to ascribe the predicate Q*

From *Philosophical Studies*, vol. 6, 1955. Reprinted by permission of the *Philosophical Studies* and the author.

to y." For Carnap, in order for P to be the intension of Q in language L for L-language user X at time t, X must have the disposition of ascribing Q to any object y if and only if y has the property P (Py) at time t. Following this treatment, Carnap arrives at criteria for sameness of intension and universal intension, in other words, synonymity and analyticity.

To indicate the value of the intensionalist thesis, Carnap asks us to consider the case of two linguists who are writing German-English dictionaries who examine the language behavior of German-speaking Karl. After examining Karl's behavior and after coming to a complete agreement as to the extension of Pferd in Karl's vocabulary, these linguists proceed to make entries into their German-English dictionaries. One linguist writes

(a) Pferd, horse,

while the other writes

(b) Pferd, horse or unicorn.

If the extensionalists are right, there is no way of deciding which of (a) and (b) is right. Indeed, there would be no difference between (a) and (b) on the extensionalist's position. But according to Carnap, there is a difference between (a) and (b), and the clue to discovering this difference is to be found not only in examining the behavior of Karl in the application of these words in the actual cases in which they apply but in examining Karl's behavior about the possible cases of their applications.

It is well known that Quine is no lover of modalities, and discussion of possible cases requires a defense of modalities which Carnap has given elsewhere. Carnap appears to attempt to keep the ontological problem involving unicorns completely divorced from the problem of determining the intension of 'unicorn.' * Whether he succeeds, however, is doubtful. Carnap advocates talking about hypothetical situations and saying to Karl, "If such and such a creature did exist would you call it a unicorn?" Carnap seems to think that most people (including Quine) are able

---

° For further comment by Carnap on the determining of intensions by empirical procedures see his "Quine on Logical Truth," P. A. Schilpp, *The Philosophy of Rudolf Carnap* (LaSalle, Ill.: Open Court Publishing Co., 1963), pp. 919 ff.

*to understand artificially constructed situations. However, the difficulties raised in recent literature regarding the analysis of contrary-to-fact hypotheticals warrant a closer look at Carnap's possible cases of applications of words. Finally, one may ask whether the construction of possible uses of language could ever ascertain whether a particular language user regarded two terms as coextensional or synonymous.*

### 1. MEANING ANALYSIS IN PRAGMATICS AND SEMANTICS

The analysis of meanings of expressions occurs in two fundamentally different forms. The first belongs to *pragmatics*, that is, the empirical investigation of historically given *natural languages*. This kind of analysis has long been carried out by linguists and philosophers, especially analytic philosophers. The second form was developed only recently in the field of symbolic logic; this form belongs to *semantics* (here understood in the sense of pure semantics, while descriptive semantics may be regarded as part of pragmatics), that is, the study of constructed *language systems* given by their rules.

The theory of the relations between a language—either a natural language or a language system—and what language is about may be divided into two parts which I call the theory of extension and the theory of intension, respectively.[1] The first deals with concepts like denoting, naming, extension, truth, and related ones. (For example, the word 'blau' in German, and likewise the predicate "*B*" in a symbolic language system if a rule assigns to it the same meaning, denote any object that is blue; its extension is the class of all blue objects; 'der Mond' is a name of the moon; the sentence 'der Mond ist blau' is true if and only if the moon is blue.) The theory of intension deals with concepts like intension, synonymy, analyticity, and related ones; for our present discussion let us call them "*inten-*

---

1. This distinction is closely related to that between radical concepts and L-concepts which I made in *Introduction to Semantics*. The contrast between extension and intension is the basis of the semantical method which I developed in *Meaning and Necessity*. Quine calls the two theories "theory of reference" and "theory of meaning," respectively.

*sion concepts.*" (I use 'intension' as a technical term for the meaning of an expression or, more specifically, for its designative meaning component; see below. For example, the intension of 'blau' in German is the property of being blue; two predicates are synonymous if and only if they have the same intension; a sentence is analytic if it is true by virtue of the intensions of the expressions occurring in it.)

From a systematic point of view, the description of a language may well begin with the theory of intension and then build the theory of extension on its basis. By learning the theory of intension of a language, say German, we learn the intensions of the words and phrases and finally of the sentences. Thus the theory of intension of a given language $L$ enables us to *understand* the sentences of $L$. On the other hand, we can apply the concepts of the theory of extension of $L$ only if we have, in addition to the knowledge of the theory of intension of $L$, also sufficient empirical knowledge of the relevant facts. For example, in order to ascertain whether a German word denotes a given object, one must first understand the word, that is, know what is its intension, in other words, know the general condition which an object must fulfill in order to be denoted by this word; and secondly he must investigate the object in question in order to see whether it fulfills the condition or not. On the other hand, if a linguist makes an empirical investigation of a language not previously described, he finds out first that certain objects are denoted by a given word, and later he determines the intension of the word.

Nobody doubts that the pragmatical investigation of natural languages is of greatest importance for an understanding both of the behavior of individuals and of the character and development of whole cultures. On the other hand, I believe with the majority of logicians today that for the special purpose of the development of logic the construction and semantical investigation of language systems are more important. But also for the logician a study of pragmatics may be useful. If he wishes to find out an efficient form for a language system to be used, say, in a branch of empirical science, he might find fruitful suggestions by a study of the natural development of the language of scientists and even of the everyday language. Many of the concepts used today in pure semantics were indeed suggested by corresponding pragmatical concepts which had been used for natural languages by philosophers or linguists, though usually without exact definitions. Those semantical concepts were, in a sense, intended as explicata for the corresponding pragmatical concepts.

In the case of the semantical intension concepts there is an additional motivation for studying the corresponding pragmatical concepts. The reason is that some of the objections raised against these semantical concepts concern, not so much any particular proposed explication, but the question of the very existence of the alleged explicanda. Especially *Quine's* criticism does not concern the formal correctness of the definitions in pure semantics; rather, he doubts whether there are any clear and fruitful corresponding pragmatical concepts which could serve as explicanda. That is the reason why he demands that these pragmatical concepts be shown to be scientifically legitimate by stating empirical, behavioristic criteria for them. If I understand him correctly, he believes that, without this pragmatical substructure, the semantical intension concepts, even if formally correct, are arbitrary and without purpose. I do not think that a semantical concept, in order to be fruitful, must necessarily possess a prior pragmatical counterpart. It is theoretically possible to demonstrate its fruitfulness through its application in the further development of language systems. But this is a slow process. If for a given semantical concept there is already a familiar, though somewhat vague, corresponding pragmatical concept and if we are able to clarify the latter by describing an operational procedure for its application, then this may indeed be a simpler way for refuting the objections and furnish a practical justification at once for both concepts.

The purpose of this paper is to clarify the nature of the pragmatical concept of intension in natural languages and to outline a behavioristic, operational procedure for it. This will give a practical vindication for the semantical intension concepts; ways for defining them, especially analyticity, I have shown in a previous paper.[2] By way of introduction I shall first (in §2) discuss briefly the pragmatical concepts of denotation and extension; it seems to be generally agreed that they are scientifically legitimate.

## 2. THE DETERMINATION OF EXTENSIONS

We take as example the German language. We imagine that a linguist who does not know anything about this language sets out to study it by observing the linguistic behavior of German-speaking people. More specifically, he studies the German language as used by a given person Karl at a given time. For simplicity, we restrict the discussion in this paper mainly to predicates applicable to observable things, like 'blau' and 'Hund.' It is generally agreed that, on the basis of spontaneous or elicited utterances of a person, the linguist can ascertain whether or not the person is willing to apply a certain predicate to a given thing, in other words, whether the predicate denotes the given thing for the person. By collecting results of this kind, the linguist can determine first, the extension of the predicate 'Hund' within a given region for Karl, that is, the class of the things to which Karl is willing to apply the predicate, second, the extension of the contradictory, that is, the class of those things for which Karl denies the application of 'Hund,' and, third, the intermediate class of those things for which Karl is not willing either to affirm or to deny the predicate. The size of the third class indicates the degree of vagueness of the predicate 'Hund,' if we disregard for simplicity the effect of Karl's ignorance about relevant facts. For certain predicates, for example, 'Mensch,' this third class is relatively very small; the degree of their extensional vagueness is low. On the basis of the determination of the three classes for the predicate "Hund" within the investigated region, the linguist may make a hypothesis concerning the responses of Karl to things outside of that region, and maybe even a hypothesis concerning the total extension in

2. R. Carnap, "Meaning Postulates," *Philosophical Studies*, 3 (1952): 65–73.

the universe. The latter hypothesis cannot, of course, be completely verified, but every single instance of it can in principle be tested. On the other hand, it is also generally agreed that this determination of extension involves uncertainty and possible error. But since this holds for all concepts of empirical science, nobody regards this fact as a sufficient reason for rejecting the concepts of the theory of extension. The sources of uncertainty are chiefly the following: first, the linguist's acceptance of the result that a given thing is denoted by 'Hund' for Karl may be erroneous, for example, due to a misunderstanding or a factual error of Karl's; and, second, the generalization to things which he has not tested suffers, of course, from the uncertainty of all inductive inference.

### 3. THE DETERMINATION OF INTENSIONS

The purpose of this paper is to defend the thesis that the analysis of intension for a natural language is a scientific procedure, methodologically just as sound as the analysis of extension. To many linguists and philosophers this thesis will appear as a truism. However, some contemporary philosophers, especially Quine [3] and White,[4] believe that the pragmatical intension concepts are foggy, mysterious, and not really understandable, and that so far no explications for them have been given. They believe further that, if an explication for one of these concepts is found, it will at best be in the form of a concept of degree. They acknowledge the good scientific status of the pragmatical concepts of the theory of extension. They emphasize that their objection against the intension concepts is based on a point of principle and not on the generally recognized facts of the technical difficulty of linguistic investigations, the inductive uncertainty, and the vagueness of the words of ordinary language. I shall therefore leave aside in my discussion these difficulties, especially the two mentioned at the end of the last section. Thus

3. W. V. Quine, *From a Logical Point of View: Nine Logico-Philosophical Essays* (1953). For his criticism of intension concepts see especially Essays II ("Two Dogmas of Empiricism," first published in 1951), III, and VII.

4. M. White, "The Analytic and the Synthetic: An Untenable Dualism" in Sidney Hook, ed., *John Dewey: Philosopher of Science and Freedom,* 1950, pp. 316–30.

the question is this: *granted that the linguist can determine the extension of a given predicate, how can he go beyond this and determine also its intension?*

The technical term 'intension,' which I use here instead of the ambiguous word 'meaning,' is meant to apply only to the cognitive or designative meaning component. I shall not try to define this component. It was mentioned earlier that determination of truth presupposes knowledge of meaning (in addition to knowledge of facts); now, cognitive meaning may be roughly characterized as that meaning component which is relevant for the determination of truth. The noncognitive meaning components, although irrelevant for questions of truth and logic, may still be very important for the psychological effect of a sentence on a listener, for example, by emphasis, emotional associations, motivational effects.

It must certainly be admitted that the pragmatical determination of intensions involves a new step and therefore a new methodological problem. Let us assume that two linguists, investigating the language of Karl, have reached complete agreement in the determination of the extension of a given predicate in a given region. This means that they agree for everything in this region, whether or not the predicate in question denotes it for Karl or not. As long as only these results are given, no matter how large the region is—you may take it, fictitiously, as the whole world, if you like—it is still possible for the linguists to ascribe to the predicate different intensions. For there are more than one and possibly infinitely many properties whose extension within the given region is just the extension determined for the predicate.

Here we come to the core of the controversy. It concerns the nature of a linguist's assignment of one of these properties to the predicate as its intension. This assignment may be made explicit by an entry in the German-English dictionary, conjoining the German predicate with an English phrase. The linguist declares hereby the German predicate to be synonymous with the English phrase. The *intensionalist thesis* in pragmatics, which I am defending, says that the assignment of an intension is an empirical hypothesis which, like any other hypothesis in linguistics, can be tested by observations of language behavior. On the other hand, *the extensionalist thesis* asserts that the assignment of an intension, on the basis of the previously determined extension is not a question of fact but merely a matter of choice. The thesis holds that the linguist is free to choose any of those properties which fit to the given extension; he may be guided in his choice by a consideration of simplicity, but there is no question of right or wrong. Quine seems to maintain this thesis; he says: "The finished lexicon is a case evidently of *ex pede Herculem*. But there is a difference. In projecting Hercules from the foot we risk error but we may derive comfort from the fact that there is something to be wrong about. In the case of the lexicon, pending some definition of synonymy, we have no stating of the problem; we have nothing for the lexicographer to be right or wrong about." ( Quine, *Logical Point of View*, p. 63.)

I shall now plead for the intensionalist thesis. Suppose, for example, that one linguist, after an investigation of Karl's speaking behavior, writes into his dictionary the following:

(1) *Pferd*, horse,

while another linguist writes:

(2) *Pferd*, horse or unicorn.

Since there are no unicorns, the two intensions ascribed to the word "Pferd" by the two linguists, although different, have the same extension. If the extensionalist thesis were right, here would be no way for empirically deciding beween (1) and (2). Since the extension is the same, no response by Karl, affirmative or negative, with respect to any actual thing can make a difference between (1) and (2). But what else is there to investigate for the linguist beyond Karl's responses concerning the application of the predicate to all the cases that can be found? The answer is, he must take into account not only the actual cases, but also possible cases.[5] The most direct way of doing this would be for

5. Some philosophers have indeed defined the intension of a predicate (or a concept closely related to it) as the class of the possible objects falling under it. For example, C. I. Lewis defines: "The comprehension of a term is the classification of all consistently thinkable things to which the

the linguist to use, in the German questions directed to Karl, modal expressions corresponding to "possible case" or the like. To be sure, these expressions are usually rather ambiguous; but this difficulty can be overcome by giving suitable explanations and examples. I do not think that there is any objection of principle against the use of modal terms. On the other hand, I think that their use is not necessary. The linguist could simply describe for Karl cases, which he knows to be possible, and leave it open whether there is anything satisfying those descriptions or not. He may, for example, describe a unicorn (in German) by something corresponding to the English formulation: "a thing similar to a horse, but having only one horn in the middle of the forehead." Or he may point toward a thing and then describe the intended modification in words, for example, "a thing like this one but having one horn in the middle of the forehead." Or, finally, he might just point to a picture representing a unicorn. Then he asks Karl whether he is willing to apply the word 'Pferd' to a thing of this kind. An affirmative or a negative answer will constitute a confirming instance for (2) or (1) respectively. This shows that (1) and (2) are different empirical hypotheses.

All *logically possible* cases come into consideration for the determination of intensions. This includes also those cases that are causally impossible, that is, excluded by the laws of nature holding in our universe, and certainly those that are excluded by laws which Karl believes to hold. Thus, if Karl believes that all $P$ are $Q$ by a law of nature, the linguist will still induce him to consider things that are $P$ but not $Q$, and ask him whether or not he would apply to them the predicate under investigation (e.g., 'Pferd').

The inadequacy of the extensionalist thesis is also shown by

---

term would correctly apply" ("The Modes of Meaning," *Philosophy and Phenomenological Research*, 4 [1944]: 236–50). I prefer to apply modalities like possibility not to objects but only to intensions, especially to propositions or to properties (kinds). (Compare *Meaning and Necessity*, pp. 66 f.) To speak of a possible case means to speak of a kind of objects which is possibly non-empty.

the following example. Consider, on the one hand, these customary entries in German-English dictionaries:

(3) *Einhorn,* unicorn. *Kobold,* goblin,

and, on the other hand, the following unusual entries:

(4) *Einhorn,* goblin. *Kobold,* unicorn.

Now the two German words (and likewise the two English words) have the same extension, namely, the null class. Therefore, if the extensionalist thesis were correct, there would be no essential, empirically testable difference between (3) and (4). The extensionalist is compelled to say that the fact that (3) is generally accepted and (4) generally rejected is merely due to a tradition created by the lexicographers, and that there are no facts of German language behavior which could be regarded as evidence in favor of (3) as against (4). I wonder whether any linguist would be willing to accept (4). Or, to avoid the possibly misguiding influence of the lexicographers' tradition, let us put the question this way: would a man on the street, who has learned both languages by practical use without lessons or dictionaries, accept as correct a translation made according to (4)?

In general terms, the determination of the intension of a predicate may start from some instances denoted by the predicate. The essential task is then to find out what variations of a given specimen in various respects (e.g., size, shape, color) are admitted within the range of the predicate. The intension of a predicate may be defined as its range, which comprehends those possible kinds of objects for which the predicate holds. In this investigation of intension, the linguist finds a new kind of vagueness, which may be called *intensional vagueness.* As mentioned above, the extensional vagueness of the word 'Mensch' is very small, at least in the accessible region. First, the intermediate zone among animals now living on earth is practically empty. Second, if the ancestors of man are considered, it is probably found that Karl cannot easily draw a line; thus there is an intermediate zone, but it is relatively small. However, when the linguist proceeds to the determination of the *intension* of the word 'Mensch,' the situation is quite different. He has to test Karl's responses to descriptions of strange kinds of animals, say intermediate between man and dog, man and lion, man and hawk, etc. It may be that the linguist and Karl know that these kinds of animals have never lived on earth; they do not know whether or not these kinds will ever occur on earth or on any other planet in any galaxy. At any rate, this knowledge or ignorance is irrelevant for the determination of intension. But Karl's ignorance has the psychological effect that he has seldom if ever thought of these kinds (unless he happens to be a student of mythology or a science-fiction fan) and therefore never felt an urge to make up his mind to which of them to apply the predicate 'Mensch.' Consequently, the linguist finds in Karl's responses a large intermediate zone for this predicate, in other words, a high intensional vagueness. The fact that Karl has not made such decisions means that the intension of the word 'Mensch' for him is not quite clear even to himself, that he does not completely understand his own word. This lack of clarity does not bother him much because it holds only for aspects which have very little practical importance for him.

The extensionalist will perhaps reject as impracticable the described procedure for determining intensions because, he might say, the man on the street is unwilling to say anything about nonexistent objects. If Karl happens to be over-realistic in this way, the linguist could still resort to a lie, reporting, say, his alleged observations of unicorns. But this is by no means necessary. The tests concerning intensions are independent of questions of existence. The man on the street is very well able to understand and to answer questions about assumed situations, where it is left open whether anything of the kind described will ever actually occur or not, and even about nonexisting situations. This is shown in ordinary conversations about alternative plans of action, about the truth of reports, about dreams, legends, and fairy tales.

Although I have given here only a rough indication of the empirical procedure for determining intensions, I believe that it is sufficient to make clear that it would be possible to write along the lines indicated a manual for determining intensions or, more exactly, for testing hypotheses concerning intensions. The kinds of rules in such a manual would not be essentially different from those customarily given for procedures in psychology, linguistics, and anthropology. Therefore the rules could be understood and carried out by any scientist (provided he is not infected by philosophical prejudices).[6]

### 4. INTENSIONS IN THE LANGUAGE OF SCIENCE

The discussions in this paper concern in general a simple, prescientific language, and the predicates considered designate observable properties of material bodies. Let us now briefly take a look at the *language of science*. It is today still mainly a natural language (except for its mathematical part), with only a few explicitly made conventions for some special words or symbols. It is a variant of the prescientific language, caused by special professional needs. The degree of precision is here in general considerably higher (i.e., the degree of vagueness is lower) than in the everyday language, and this degree is continually increasing. It is important to note that this increase

6. After writing the present paper I have become acquainted with a very interesting new book by Arne Naess, *Interpretation and Preciseness: A Contribution to the Theory of Communication* (Skrifter Norske Vid. Akademi, Oslo, II. Hist.-Filos. Klasse, 1953, No. 1). This book describes in detail various procedures for testing hypotheses concerning the synonymity of expressions with the help of questionnaires, and gives examples of statistical results found with these questionnaires. The practical difficulties and sources of possible errors are carefully investigated. The procedures concern the responses of the test persons, not to observed objects as in the present paper, but to pairs of sentences within specified contexts. Therefore the questions are formulated in the metalanguage, for example, "Do the two given sentences in the given context express the same assertion to you?" Although there may be different opinions concerning some features of the various procedures, it seems to me that the book marks an important progress in the methodology of empirical meaning analysis for natural languages. Some of the questions used refer also to possible kinds of cases, for example, "Can you imagine circumstances (conditions, situations) in which you would accept the one sentence and reject the other, or vice versa?" (p. 368). The book, both in its methodological discussions and in its reports on experiences with the questionnaires, seems to me to provide abundant evidence in support of the intensionalist thesis (in the sense explained in §3 above).

holds not only for extensional but also for intensional precision; that is to say that not only the extensional intermediate zones (i.e., those of actual occurrences) but also the intensional ones (i.e., those of possible occurrences) are shrinking. In consequence of this development, also, the intension concepts become applicable with increasing clarity. In the oldest books on chemistry, for example, there were a great number of statements describing the properties of a given substance, say water or sulphuric acid, including its reactions with other substances. There was no clear indication as to which of these numerous properties were to be taken as essential or definitory for the substance. Therefore, at least on the basis of the book alone, we cannot determine which of the statements made in the book were analytic and which synthetic for its author. The situation was similar with books on zoology, even at at much later time; we find a lot of statements, for example, on the lion, without a clear separation of the definitory properties. But in chemistry there was an early development from the state described to states of greater and greater intensional precision. On the basis of the theory of chemical elements, slowly with increasing explicitness certain properties were selected as essential. For a compound, the molecular formula (e.g., '$H_2O$') was taken as definitory, and later the molecular structure diagram. For the elementary substances, first certain experimental properties were more and more clearly selected as definitory, for example the atomic weight, later the position in Mendeleyev's system. Still later, with a differentiation of the various isotopes, the nuclear composition was regarded as definitory, say characterized by the number of protons (atomic number) and the number of neutrons.

We can at the present time observe the advantages already obtained by the explicit conventions which have been made, though only to a very limited extent, in the language of empirical science, and the very great advantages effected by the moderate measure of formalization in the language of mathematics. Let us suppose—as I indeed believe, but that is outside of our present discussion—that this trend toward explicit rules will continue. Then the practical question arises whether rules of extension are sufficient or whether it would be advisable to lay down also rules of intension? In my view, it follows from the previous discussion that rules of intension are required, because otherwise intensional vagueness would remain, and this would prevent clear mutual understanding and effective communication.

### 5. THE GENERAL CONCEPT OF THE INTENSION OF A PREDICATE

We have seen that there is an empirical procedure for testing, by observations of linguistic behavior, a hypothesis concerning the intension of a predicate, says 'Pferd,' for a speaker, says Karl. Since a procedure of this kind is applicable to any hypothesis of intension, the general concept of the intension of any predicate in any language for any person at any time has a clear, empirically testable sense. This general concept of intension may be characterized roughly as follows, leaving subtleties aside: the intension of the predicate '$Q$' for a speaker $X$ is the general condition which an object $y$ must fulfill in order for $X$ to be willing to ascribe the predicate '$Q$' to $y$. (We omit, for simplicity, the reference to a time $t$.) Let us try to make this general characterization more explicit. That $X$ is able to use a langauge $L$ means that $X$ has a certain system of interconnected dispositions for certain linguistic responses. That the predicate '$Q$' in a language $L$ has the property $F$ as its intension for $X$, means that among the dispositions of $X$ constituting the language $L$ there is the disposition of ascribing the predicate '$Q$' to any object $y$ if and only if $y$ has the property $F$. ($F$ is here always assumed to be an observable property, that is, either directly observable or explicitly definable in terms of directly observable properties.) (The given formulation is oversimplified, neglecting vagueness. In order to take vagueness into account, a pair of intentions $F_1$, $F_2$ must be stated: $X$ has the disposition of ascribing affirmatively the predicate '$Q$' to an object $y$ if and only if $y$ has $F_1$; and the disposition of denying '$Q$' for $y$ if and only if $y$ has $F_2$. Thus, if $y$ has neither $F_1$ nor $F_2$, $X$ will give neither an affirmative nor a negative response; the property of having neither $F_1$ nor $F_2$ constitutes the zone of vagueness, which may possibly be empty.)

The concept of intension has here been characterized only for thing-predicates. The characterization for expressions of other types, including sentences, can be given in an analogous way. The other concepts of the theory of intension can then be defined in the usual way; we shall state only those for 'synonymous' and 'analytic' in a simple form without claim to exactness.

Two expressions are *synonymous* in the language $L$ for $X$ at time $t$ if they have the same intension in $L$ for $X$ at $t$.

A sentence is *analytic* in $L$ for $X$ at $t$ if its intension (or range or truth-condition) in $L$ for $X$ at $t$ comprehends all possible cases.

A language $L$ was characterized above as a system of certain dispositions for the use of expressions. I shall now make some remarks on the *methodology of dispositional concepts*. This will help to a clearer understanding of the nature of linguistic concepts in general and of the concept of intension in particular. Let $D$ be the disposition of $X$ to react to a condition $C$ by the characteristic response $R$. There are in principle, although not always in practice, two ways for ascertaining whether a given thing or person $X$ has the disposition $D$ (at a given time $t$). The first method may be called *behavioristic* (in a very wide sense); it consists in producing the condition $C$ and then determining whether or not the response $R$ occurs. The second way may be called the *method of structure analysis*. It consists in investigating the state of $X$ (at $t$) in sufficient detail such that it is possible to derive from the obtained description of the state with the help of relevant general laws (say of physics, physiology, etc.) the responses which $X$ would make to any specified circumstances in the environment. Then it will be possible to predict, in particular, whether under the condition $C$ $X$ would make the response $R$ or not; if so, $X$ has the disposition $D$, otherwise not. For example, let $X$ be an automobile and $D$ be the ability for a specified acceleration on a horizontal road at a speed of 10 miles per hour. The hypothesis that the automobile has this ability $D$ may be tested by either of the following two procedures. The behavioristic method consists in driving the car and observing its performance under the specified conditions. The second method consists in studying the internal structure of the car, especially the motor, and calculating with the help of physical laws the acceleration which would result under the specified conditions. With respect to a psychological disposition and, in particular, a linguistic disposition of a person $X$, there is first the familiar behavioristic method and second, at least theoretically, the method of a micro-physiological investigation of the body of $X$, especially the central nervous system. At the present state of physiological knowledge of the human organism and especially the central nervous system, the second method is, of course, not practicable.

### 6. THE CONCEPT OF INTENSION FOR A ROBOT

In order to make the method of structure analysis applicable, let us now consider the pragmatical investigation of the language of a robot rather than that of a human being. In this case we may assume that we possess much more detailed knowledge of the internal structure. The logical nature of the pragmatical concepts remains just the same. Suppose that we have a sufficiently detailed blueprint according to which the robot $X$ was constructed and that $X$ has abilities of observation and of use of language. Let us assume that $X$ has three input organs $A$, $B$, and $C$, and an output organ. $A$ and $B$ are used alternatively, never simultaneously. $A$ is an organ of visual observation of objects presented. $B$ can receive a general description of a kind of object (a predicate expression) in the language $L$ of $X$, which may consist of written marks or of holes punched in a card. $C$ receives a predicate. These inputs constitute the question whether the object presented at $A$ or any object satisfying the description presented at $B$ is denoted in $L$ for $X$ by the predicate presented at $C$. The output organ may then supply one of three responses of $X$, for affirmation, denial, or abstention; the latter response would be given, for example, if the observation of the object at $A$ or the description at $B$ were not sufficient to determine a definite answer. Just as the linguist investigating Karl begins with pointing to objects, but later, after having determined the interpretation of some words, asks questions formulated by these words, the investigator of $X$'s language $L$ begins with presenting objects at *A*, but later, on the basis of tentative results concerning the intensions of some signs of *L*, proceeds to present predicate expressions at *B* which use only those interpreted signs and not the predicate presented at *C*.

Instead of using this behavioristic method, the investigator may here use the method of structure analysis. On the basis of the given blueprint of *X*, he may be able to calculate the responses which *X* would make to various possible inputs. In particular, he may be able to derive from the given blueprint, with the help of those laws of physics which determine the functioning of the organs of *X*, the following result with respect to a given predicate '*Q*' of the language *L* of *X* and specified properties $F_1$ and $F_2$ (observable for *X*): If the predicate '*Q*' is presented at *C*, then *X* gives an affirmative response if and only if an object having the property $F_1$ is presented at *A* and a negative response if and only if an object with $F_2$ is presented at *A*. This result indicates that the boundary of the intension of '*Q*' is somewhere between the boundary of $F_1$ and that of $F_2$. For some predicates the zone of indeterminateness between $F_1$ and $F_2$ may be fairly small and hence this preliminary determination of the intension fairly precise. This might be the case, for example, for color predicates if the investigator has a sufficient number of color specimens.

After this preliminary determination of the intensions of some predicates constituting a restricted vocabulary *V* by calculations concerning input *A*, the investigator will proceed to making calculations concerning descriptions containing the predicates of *V* to be presented at *B*. He may be able to derive from the blueprint the following result: If the predicate '*P*' is presented at *C*, and any description *D* in terms of the vocabulary *V* is presented at *B*, *X* gives an affirmative response if and only if *D* (as interpreted by the preliminary results) logically implies $G_1$, and a negative response if and only if *D* logically implies $G_2$. This result indicates that the boundary of the intension of '*P*' is between the boundary of $G_1$ and that of $G_2$. In this way more precise determinations for a more comprehensive part of *L* and finally for the whole of *L* may be obtained. (Here again we assume that the predicates of $L$ designate observable properties of things.)

It is clear that the method of structure analysis, if applicable, is more powerful than the behavioristic method, because it can supply a general answer and, under favorable circumstances, even a complete answer to the question of the intension of a given predicate.

Note that the procedure described for input $A$ can include empty kinds of objects and the procedure for input $B$ even causally impossible kinds. Thus, for example, though we cannot present a unicorn at $A$, we can nevertheless calculate which response $X$ would make if a unicorn were presented at $A$. This calculation is obviously in no way affected by any zoological fact concerning the existence or nonexistence of unicorns. The situation is different for a kind of objects excluded by a law of physics, especially, a law needed in the calculations about the robot. Take the law $l_1$: "Any iron body at 6o° F is solid." The investigator needs this law in his calculation of the functioning of $X$, in order to ascertain that some iron cogwheels do not melt. If now he were to take as a premise for his derivation the statement "A liquid iron body having the temperature of 6o° F is presented at $A$," then, since the law $l_1$ belongs also to his premises, he would obtain a contradiction; hence every statement concerning $X$'s response would be derivable, and thus the method would break down. But even for this case the method still works with respect to $B$. He may take as premise "The description 'liquid iron body with the temperature of 6o° F' (that is, the translation of this into $L$) is presented at $B$." Then no contradiction arises either in the derivation made by the investigator or in that made by $X$. *The derivation carried out by the investigator* contains the premise just mentioned, which does not refer to an iron body but to a description, say a card punched in a certain way; thus there is no contradiction, although the law $l_1$ occurs also as a premise. On the other hand, in *the derivation made by the robot* $X$, the card presented at $B$ supplies, as it were, a premise of the form "$y$ is a liquid iron body at 6o° F"; but here the law $l_1$ does not occur as a premise, and thus no contradiction occurs. $X$ makes merely logical deductions from the one premise stated and, if the predicate '$R$' is presented at $C$, tries to come either to the conclusion "$y$ is $R$" or "$y$ is not $R$." Suppose the investigator's calculation leads to the result that $X$ would derive the conclusion "$y$ is $R$" and hence that $X$ would give an affirmative response. This result would show that the (causally impossible) kind of liquid iron bodies at 60° F is included in the range of the intension of '$R$' for $X$.

I have tried to show in this paper that in a pragmatical investigation of a natural language there is not only, as generally agreed, an empirical method for ascertaining which objects are denoted by a given predicate and thus for determining the extension of the predicate, but also a method for testing a hypothesis concerning its intension (designative meaning).[7] The intension of a predicate for a speaker $X$ is, roughly speaking, the general condition which an object must fulfill for $X$ to be willing to apply the predicate to it. For the determination of intension, not only actually given cases must be taken into consideration, but also possible cases, that is, kinds of objects which can be described without self-contradiction, irrespective of the question whether there are any objects of the kinds described. The intension of a predicate can be determined for a robot just as well as for a human speaker, and even more completely if the internal structure of the robot is sufficiently known to predict how it will function under various conditions. On the basis of the concept of intension, other pragmatical concepts with respect to

7. Y. Bar-Hillel in a recent paper ("Logical Syntax and Semantics," *Language* 30 [1954]: 230–37) defends the concept of meaning against those contemporary linguists who wish to ban it from linguistics. He explains this tendency by the fact that in the first quarter of this century the concept of meaning was indeed in a bad methodological state; the usual explanations of the concept involved psychologistic connotations, which were correctly criticized by Bloomfield and others. Bar-Hillel points out that the semantical theory of meaning developed recently by logicians is free of these drawbacks. He appeals to the linguists to construct in an analogous way the theory of meaning needed in their empirical investigations. The present paper indicates the possibility of such a construction. The fact that the concept of intension can be applied even to a robot shows that it does not have the psychologistic character of the traditional concept of meaning.

natural languages can be defined, synonymy, analyticity, and the like. The existence of scientifically sound pragmatical concepts of this kind provides a practical motivation and justification for the introduction of corresponding concepts in pure semantics with respect to constructed language systems.

# ANALYTIC-SYNTHETIC

## Jonathan Bennett

*Bennett holds that an attack on "Two Dogmas" is still needed. For a blend of the destructive and constructive arguments of that article form an argument against most of the defenses of the traditional distinction which "Two Dogmas" provoked. This blend would make it possible to explain the distinction without using any intensional notions, and thus undercut most of Quine's critics. Bennett uses resources suggested in the terminal section of "Two Dogmas" to construct a Quinean theory of the analytic-synthetic distinction. Employing the notion of the relative indispensability of sentences, he explains the distinction, without, at least superficially using any intensional idioms; the analytic sentences turn out to be the most indispensable at a given time. This makes the distinction a matter of difference in degree, rather than difference in kind, a result which presumably Quine*

From *The Proceedings of the Aristotelian Society,* vol. 54, 1958–9. Reprinted by permission of The Aristotelian Society and the author.

*would welcome. Bennett counters the objection that according to this theory a statement can be both analytic and false with the retort that the objection depends upon a distinction which is intensional. To the objection that this theory is too limited, Bennett replies, in effect, that expanding the theory would be a dubious business.*

*The Quinean theory thus erected consists of a positive and a negative thesis; the former, the workaday employment of the analytic-synthetic distinction can be understood in terms of degrees of indispensability; the latter, none of the arguments which have so far appeared in the literature succeeds in showing that there is any reason for treating the analytic-synthetic distinction in a quite different way, such that it can be called a distinction in kind rather than in degree.*

*The remainder of Bennett's article consists in a pitting of Bennett's Quinean theory against the traditional theory, and terminates with the presentation of a non-Quinean theory of the analytic-synthetic distinction. There is not space here to summarize these sections at all adequately. So the reader is left on his own—it being the wiser not to attempt the impossible. But perhaps enough has been said to indicate the general direction of Bennett's thought.*

*Some questions which are prompted by Bennett's article are the following: The special merit which Bennett claims for his interpretation of the Quinean theory of the analytic-synthetic distinction is that it provides a stronger criticism of the traditional distinction in that it provides an explanation of that distinction which could be understood by someone who had no understanding of any intensional terminology at all. Bennett's Quinean theory therefore does not depend upon the Quinean argument to the effect that intensional notions are not sufficiently understood, this being the focus of much of the critical writing against Quine. But could it not be that Bennett's notion of indispensability—upon which his account of the distinction turns—is itself intensional? Could it be any more fully explained or analyzed without the introduction of some or other intensional notion? Are not the notions of acceptance and of dependence, which are prominent in Bennett's account of indis-*

*pensability, themselves intensional? In short, has Bennett in fact
succeeded in constructing a non-intensional explanation of the
Quinean theory of the analytic-synthetic distinction?*

## 1. INTRODUCTORY

This paper attacks Quine's views on the analytic-synthetic distinction (ASD), first arguing that an attack is still required.
This preliminary thesis is based on the claim that what Quine
presents as (1) an attack on the ASD, followed by (2) some remarks about confirmation and disconfirmation, offers a more
formidable obstacle to the adherent of the traditional ASD if
(2) is built into (1) as a positive but unwelcome theory of the
ASD.

I shall argue that a proponent of this broadly Quinean theory
of the ASD has a crucial advantage over most of Quine's critics
who have so far published,[1] namely that if the Quinean theory
is correct then it is possible clearly and cogently to explain the
ASD to someone who does not yet understand any intensional
terminology at all. I shall try to give such an explanation in
terms of the Quinean theory, and to show that there are some
grounds for pessimism as to the chances of the rival theory's
being able to do as well. Formal definitions of intensional terms
always involve other intensional terms, of course, but I shall
argue that *any* of the usual non-Quinean ways of explaining intensional terminology, however informally, essentially involve a
prior understanding of other intensional terms.

Grice and Strawson ("Defense of Dogma," p. 151) offer one
such explanation, freely admit that it is not a *full* explanation of
the intensional term concerned, but claim that at least 'it breaks
out of the family-circle [of intensional terms].' I shall argue
that this is not true. But this leaves open the question whether
they would grant that the provision of explanations which break

1. Of the many articles defending the traditional point of view, I shall
be almost exclusively concerned with the most considerable, H. G. Grice
and P. F. Strawson's "In Defense of a Dogma," *Philosophical Review,*
1956. But I hope also to take into account the important parts of a wide
range of talk by traditionalists in Oxford and Cambridge.

out of the family-circle is a necessary condition of the accepta-
bility of intensional terminology as a whole (and the related
question, whether they grant that the *way* in which one breaks
out of the circle must determine what theoretical remarks one
permits oneself about intensional terminology). An assumption
which will underlie the whole of this paper is that such explanations *are* required. One may of course understand a group of
words without being capable in practice of explaining their
meaning in terms of words outside the group; but if one believes
that such explanations are not even in principle available, then I
do not see how one can justifiably hold to the claim to understand the words concerned, unless one can indicate how their
meaning could be learned nonverbally (presumably through
some sort of ostensive procedure), an option which I do not
think anyone regards as open in the case of the intensional
family-circle.

### 2. A QUINEAN ANALYSIS OF THE ASD

Any given person at any given time has a corpus of belief
which is registered in a class of sentences which he calls or is
disposed to call true (or, for brevity, 'sentences which he accepts'). In the light of experience, he from time to time alters
the membership of his class of accepted sentences, because some
experiences put him in a position such that if he is to be rational
he *must* deny something he has hitherto accepted (or, for brevity, "because some experiences are recalcitrant [relative to his
class of accepted sentences]"). In making a linguistic adjustment in face of a recalcitrant experience, any given sentence
*may* be retained in the class of accepted sentences; and any
given sentence *may* be banished from that class in face of some
recalcitrant experience.

The fact that any sentence may be retained becomes obvious
upon consideration of the ways in which counter-evidence can
be explained away by the acceptance of hitherto rejected sentences (as in "The barometer must have been playing up");
and upon consideration of the fact that a sentence can always
be retained by changing its meaning appropriately. (I here use

intensional terminology, but only to point to an uncontroversial aspect of a familiar phenomenon.) Similarly, the fact that experience may lead us to reject any given sentence is just the fact that any synthetic sentence may be falsified by the empirical facts, and that any analytic sentence may become false through a meaning-change which is brought about by the occurrence of recalcitrant experiences. Some people who grant that any sentence could be rendered false by a meaning-change nevertheless claim that with only a small class of sentences is it possible to describe a state of affairs which would invite a meaning-change such as to render the sentence false. I see no reason to believe this, and as an indication of how to look for such a description in a given case, I suggest the following: associated with any analytic sentence there is a range of synthetic sentences stating facts about the world in virtue of which it is convenient that the words in the analytic sentence should have the meanings they do have; suppose a falsification of a judiciously selected subset of these synthetic sentences, and you are well on the way to describing a state of affairs which invites the falsification of the analytic sentence.

To return to our description of a range of linguistic facts which could be known and understood by someone who had no understanding of any intensional words: If two different adjustments in the face of a recalcitrant experience are envisaged, one of which produces a totality of accepted sentences which is a very great deal simpler than that resulting from the other adjustment, then the former will be chosen. The notion of simplicity used here cannot be made very precise: sometimes the greater simplicity of one totality will consist in its greater adaptability to mathematical handling; sometimes in its relative economy of basic vocabulary; sometimes in its being able to say in fewer words than the other anything that the other can say. Other criteria than simplicity also operate in these decisions, but it seems clear that wherever this criterion applies decisively in favor of one totality against another, an acceptance of the latter totality will be condemned as irrational. In some such cases it is said that the former embodies a more satisfactory conceptual scheme than the latter; in others, that certain members of the latter totality are being retained only at the cost of arbitrary and implausible saving devices of various sorts; and sometimes one would not know which of these descriptions to adopt. In the meantime we need only note the plain kind of fact which is pointed to by either description. There is a further plain fact. If someone is confronted with a recalcitrant experience, the various alternative adjustments which he may make to his hitherto accepted totality may be compared not only in respect of the simplicity of the resultant totality in each case, but also in respect of the extensiveness of the adjustment necessary to reach the resultant totality in each case. Often, if not always, the least extensive adjustment consists in dismissing the recalcitrant experience as illusory; but if this way out is taken often enough the resultant totality will be more complex— because less thoroughly organized—than would have been a totality which was more trouble to arrive at. I take an adjustment to be more extensive than another if it involves the acceptance of more hitherto rejected sentences than the other, or the rejection of more hitherto accepted sentences than the other. The two halves of this criterion do not conflict in the cases with which I am concerned.

Further: A person at a given time can have a certain amount of information about individual members of his set of accepted sentences, information as to the extensiveness of *any* adjustment of which their rejection formed a part. He will have such information about, say, the sentence $S$ if he knows that in his currently accepted set there are many sentences his acceptance of which he justifies by arguments in which $S$ occurs and which he cannot justify by arguments using only sentences he now accepts but not using $S$. For in such a case he will know that any adjustment in which $S$ is rejected will lead to a resultant totality of accepted sentences in which either (a) membership is denied to the sentences whose present defense requires $S$, or (b) membership is accorded to new sentences which provide alternative ways of justifying the continued acceptance of the sentences in question.

For example: Accepted sentences of the form (i) 'The temperature of such-and-such a star is such-and-such' depend, for

those who accept them, on sentences of the form (ii) 'Temperature correlates with light-emission in such-and-such ways,' and
these depend on sentences of the form (iii) 'Temperature correlates with mercury-column readings in such-and-such ways,'
and these in their turn depend on sentences along the lines of
(iv) 'Temperature has to do with the obtaining of such-and-such
sensations.' Rejection of (ii) jeopardizes (i) and all that depends on it; rejection of (iii) jeopardizes (i) and (ii); rejection
of (iv) jeopardizes all the other three.

This example brings out the fact that the most straightforward
cases of commensurability of two or more sentences in respect
of how much depends on them are those cases where the sentences have a general term (or an abstract noun) in common
and where one sentence is said to have more depending on it
than another simply because the second sentence itself depends
on the first. The example also helps to bring out the fact that
where $S_1$ and $S_2$ both involve a general term $F$, and where
$S_1$ depends on $S_2$, the situation can be described as one in which
$S_2$ states necessary and/or sufficient conditions for $F$ness which
are employed in establishing $S_1$. In what follows, when I wish
to say that one sentence shares a general term with another and
has more depending on it than depends on the other, I shall say
that it is *less dispensable* than the other.

Now the point of all this is that a candid observer of the
linguistic scene, having noted all these facts and having listened
to uses of intensional terminology, might very well conclude
that to call a sentence 'analytic' is to register a conviction that
it is highly indispensable—less dispensable than any sentence
which shares a general term with it and which is called 'synthetic.' It might be argued that such a belief about the meaning
of 'analytic' *must* be wrong, on the grounds that if that were
what people intend by their use of intensional terminology then
they would not make the theoretical remarks *about* intensional
terminology which in fact they do make. But if the holder of
the belief were led by it to draw the analytic-synthetic line just
where everyone else draws it, and if his critics were unable to
challenge his account of intensional terminology by producing
a counter-theory, then most of us would grant that he was en-

titled to be satisfied with his theory and to remain unconvinced by opponents' protests that his story, though extensionally adequate, was wrong in some way which they were unable to express except in words which would be intelligible only to the already converted (i.e., to those who already claimed to understand intensional terminology, and agreed that this account of it was wrong).

In fact, I cannot prove that this theory is extensionally adequate. But I do claim that it is, at least, fairly plausible: any discovery about all the $F$'s presupposes one or more tests for $F$ness (one or more answers to questions of the form 'How do you know it *was* an $F$?') and provides a new test which could be used in establishing of yet further generalizations about the $F$'s. It therefore seems reasonable to envisage a hierarchy of all the accepted sentences about the $F$'s: with the upper regions occupied by synthetic generalizations which have seldom or never provided tests for $F$ness in the establishment of other generalizations; the middle regions occupied by generalizations which are still synthetic but which—because they are better established, or longer established, or in some way more versatile —have more often been used as tools in the establishment of other generalizations; and the lower regions occupied by the analytic generalizations on which the establishment of all the others depends.

Quine does not talk about the comparative indispensability of sentences; but he does compare sentences in respect of their 'distance from the periphery' of our totality of accepted sentences, and I offer 'indispensability' as a literal version of what (I think) he is getting at with this metaphor.

Two features of the theory at present under discussion appear to give some difficulty:

(1) It has been objected that on this theory of the ASD a sentence may be analytic though false. For although 'analytic at $t_1$ is defined only for sentences accepted at $t_1$, the theory seems to allow that one might accept a sentence at $t_1$, correctly call it 'analytic' at $t_1$, reject it at $t_2$, and claim (at $t_2$) that it was false, though accepted and indeed highly indispensable, at $t_1$; whence it follows that at $t_1$ it was both analytic and false. But

this whole argument rests upon the distinction between 'S was true but is now false' and 'S was false all the time, though we thought it to be true.' This is a perfectly good distinction, of course, but it is a thoroughly intensional one: to the best of my knowledge, it can be elucidated only by means of standard intensional terminology, in such phrases as 'true with the meaning it then had, false with the meaning it now has.' An objection based on this distinction is thus illegitimate unless the objector is prepared to claim that the distinction is in some way so much clearer and plainer than the other intensional notions that once we have shown their relations with it (and they can indeed be defined in terms of it) there is nothing more that needs to be said.

(2) The theory defines the ASD only for sets of sentences having a general term in common. It draws a line, for instance, between 'Obligatory actions are permissible' on the one hand, and 'Bigamy is sometimes permissible' and 'Obligatory actions are tiresome' on the other, while cheerfully admitting that the first sentence is incommensurable with 'Some mammals are oviparous.' It has been objected that this is a difference between the ASD according to this theory and the ASD as usually drawn; for, it is said, when one says that 'Obligatory actions are permissible' is analytic while 'Some mammals are oviparous' is synthetic, one is making a distinction based on a direct comparison between these two sentences. How one takes this objection must depend upon what is meant by 'direct' comparison. Is a 'direct' contrast made between a mouse and a hamster when a nutrition researcher reports that after the first six weeks of an experiment the mouse was overgrown (i.e., larger than most mice of its age and type) while the hamster was not overgrown (i.e., not larger than most hamsters of its age and type)? If so, then the Quinean theory now under discussion *does* admit of 'direct' comparison between the members of any analytic/synthetic pair. If not, then what *is* meant by 'direct'? It seems unlikely that this point could be pressed further except as the conclusion of an argument most of which would range over more familiar territory.

The theory I am trying to elaborate appears to be unacceptable to most opponents of Quine's views on these matters. I think it is fair to say that the crucial feature to which they object is the theory's claim that the ASD marks a difference (in a quite straightforward sense) of *degree*, whereas they claim that it marks a difference (in some sense) of *kind*. Perhaps the most concrete result of this disagreement is that, according to the Quinean theory, a great deal of talk about *deciding* whether something is to be analytic or not is simply out of place. Sometimes we genuinely do not know whether a given sentence has the required degree of indispensability, and then talk about *discovery* is in order. But there is, on the Quinean theory, a large class of cases where we cannot say whether a sentence is analytic or not simply because the analytic/synthetic borderline is an indeterminate one—there just is no way of stating an exact measure of *how* much more indispensable $S$ (containing $F$) must be than most of the other sentences containing $F$ for one to call it 'analytic'—and in these cases, the Quinean theorist will say, it is inappropriate to talk (with the naïve) of discovery, and equally inappropriate to talk (with the sophisticated) of decision. There is nothing to discover, and nothing to decide.

For expository purposes I shall adopt the label 'PQ' for an imaginary proponent of the Quinean theory. PQ, then, is a man who defends the positive thesis that *the workaday employment of the ASD and related intensional terminology can be understood in terms of degrees of indispensability,* and the negative thesis that *none of the arguments which have so far appeared in the literature succeeds in showing that there is any reason for treating the ASD in quite a different way, notably in such a way that it can be called a distinction in kind rather than in degree.*

The next section will be primarily concerned with the second, negative thesis; but some of its points will be made through discussions of various sorts of challenge to PQ's positive thesis.

### 3. QUINEAN THEORY V. TRADITIONAL THEORY

The most obvious criticism to make of PQ's theory is that it is simply false, in that 'analytic' registers recognition not of some unspecified but high degree of indispensability but rather recognition that denial is not rationally possible *at all* in respect of the sentence called analytic.

This takes us over old territory. PQ's reply would be: 'But sentences universally called analytic have come to be denied in face of the facts, and any sentence now called analytic might come to suffer the same fate.' The proper response would be something like this: 'Certainly, analytic sentences have come to be said with "It is not the case that . . ." put in front of them. But in calling them analytic in the first place we were talking about the sentences with the meanings they then had; for denial to be rationally possible, the meanings had to change. Or, to put it another way, the word "analytic" strictly applies to propositions rather than to sentences; when we seem to call a sentence analytic, we are really applying the word to the proposition *then* expressed by the sentence.'

Taking up the part of this which uses the phrase 'change of meaning' and its cognates, PQ can answer as follows: 'You have added to my theory, but you have not contradicted it. For, what is it for a meaning to change? Surely, it is for a sentence, to the effect that a word applies to certain sorts of things, to have once had and no longer to have a high degree of indispensability: thus change of meaning shades into unexpectedness of application, the borderline between the two corresponding to the ASD in such a way that it is true, as you say, that the denial of a hitherto analytic sentence is the changing of a meaning. But what makes this a *criticism* of what I have been saying?'

In dealing with the part of his critic's remarks which depends on the word 'proposition,' PQ could say something like this: 'So far as I can work out this "proposition" terminology, the proposition expressed by $S_1$ at $t_1$ is different from the proposition expressed by $S_1$ at $t_2$ if and only if an appropriate set of sentences of the form "$S_1$ is true if and only if $S_n$ is true" which are highly indispensable at $t_1$ are not highly indispensable at $t_2$.[2] So that a hitherto analytic sentence can be denied only if it comes to express a different proposition from the one it formerly expressed—a conclusion which I welcome as a perfectly consistent addition to my original theory.'

This dialogue is essentially a discussion of the ASD in terms of the formal relationships holding amongst certain intensional terms. Many more could be given, threading through the network from 'proposition' to 'synonymous' to 'necessary' to 'impossible,' and so on. We know that this will achieve nothing to our present purpose for, as Quine has shown, the family is such a tightly knit one that someone who had trouble over one of its members would be likely to have trouble over all of them. In the light of PQ's positive thesis (his analysis of the ASD), however, the moral to be drawn from the smoothness of passage around the family-circle is not so much that trouble with one involves trouble with all as that a theory which is (arguably) extensionally adequate for one will be (arguably) extensionally adequate for all. And with respect to PQ's negative thesis (his, and my, critique of the standard attempts to elucidate intensional terminology as a whole), the moral is that this kind of approach will be *entirely* unhelpful to someone who does not already understand some members of the circle: if the interrelations had to be stated in a series of biconditionals which *almost* held—so that room was left for explanations, not involving intensional terminology, of some or all of the ways in which the biconditionals failed to hold exactly—then it might be useful to look to these formal relations for help. As it is, we must turn to informal explanations.

Before doing so, mention should be made of one sort of compromise of the smoothness with which intensional terms can

2. The word 'appropriate' covers some fairly complicated conditions regarding general-word-sharing between sentences. A full statement of these conditions would make it clear that sometimes we should find it difficult to say which of two groups of sentences had come to express different propositions, because we did not find it easy to say which of two general words had changed its meaning. This is not a special problem for PQ's theory, but just an observable fact about the use of intensional terminology.

be related to one another by simple biconditionals, namely the debates which break out from time to time over these biconditionals themselves: arguments over the equation of 'possibly possible' with 'possible,' of '*a priori*' with 'analytic,' of entailment with the analytic conditional, of propositional identity with reciprocal entailment, and so on. But the existence of these need not embarrass PQ, for they contain nothing on which the participants agree and the acceptance of which would create difficulties for PQ in respect of his positive thesis. Nor could such arguments be claimed to provide any illumination at all for someone who did not understand any intensional terms. Indeed, PQ could with some justice claim that the inconclusiveness of these debates points directly to the need for some such clarification of the ASD as he has offered.

I propose to consider four sorts of informal locution which are frequently used to explain in a non-question-begging way something about the way in which intensional terminology is to be used and, in particular, to give explanations which will result in the ASD's being a distinction in *kind*, in some sense incompatible with PQ's theory of the ASD. Discussion of these ways of talking will therefore be relevant to both PQ's positive and his negative theses.

(1) The whole problem would be settled in favor of PQ's opponents if a distinction in kind could be established between *factual revision* and *conceptual revision;* and it has been suggested that such a distinction begins to emerge if we consider factual *disagreements* and conceptual *disagreements*—the latter being understood as disagreements over the practical problem of which conceptual scheme to adopt—and notice that the former are always in principle capable of settlement while the latter may well go on forever without any lack of candor or energy on the part of the disputants. This suggestion, though, could well be snatched at by PQ as offering the basis for a point in his favor. For the one way in which a factual disagreement may steadily and stubbornly resist resolution is by one disputant's insisting on accommodating any evidence which tells against his thesis by the adoption of supplementary postulates of some appropriate sort; but if he does this to an enormous

degree of complexity and arbitrariness, while his opponent can defend *his* view without being driven to such shifts, it would usually be said that the former was being unreasonable and that he *should* allow the disagreement to be settled against him. And a conceptual disagreement can be settled (for all reasonable men) in all and only those situations where the adoption of one conceptual scheme has no advantage over the adoption of the other, and has the disadvantage of involving a much greater degree of complexity in what is said about the facts. The criteria for settlement of the two sorts of disputes are, in brief, identical.

It is true that when one party to a dispute persistently refuses (in the elaborate and perverse way just indicated) to lose the argument, he is often said to have turned the dispute into a 'merely conceptual' one. This way of talking suggests that in conceptual disputes the criteria for the reasonableness of a party to a factual dispute do not apply in the same way; and PQ is obliged to account for this use of 'merely conceptual.'

On his own showing, PQ is entitled to point out that someone who seems to depart from the usual criteria of reasonableness in one area of debate may naturally be assumed either to be unreasonable or to have in mind the ramifications of what he is saying into other areas altogether, and thus very likely to be concerned with the long-range benefits to be gained from the denial of one or more sentences which his opponent calls analytic. But such a man might be hoping to derive long-range benefits of simplicity at the cost of complexity in this one area, by propounding a new *scientific* theory, that is, one which challenges only sentences which would be called synthetic. If the latter is the case, then PQ must say that we are simply wrong to say 'He is turning the dispute into a merely conceptual one,' and there is an onus upon him to explain why it is that we are so ready to say this when there is always the other possibility.

An explanation, however, seems to be available: As a rule, when one is faced with a recalcitrant experience there is no time for conceptual revision (the long, hard route to an outcome) even when in the long run a conceptual revision would be the most rational move to make; and thus the standard case of conceptual revision is the situation in which there is an accommodation[3] of all the known facts, but its degree of complexity is such as to suggest (in a quiet hour) that it might be worth while to try to simplify it, if necessary the hard way. There is a tendency therefore to think of conceptual revision in terms of a move from one accommodation to another, and of factual revision in terms of the situation where one is faced with a recalcitrant experience, that is, where one does not have an accommodation of all the facts. But there is no reason in principle why a recalcitrant experience should not be given an on-the-spot accommodation which involves conceptual revision, or why an accommodation of all the known facts should not be turned quietly into something simpler by means of a factual revision.

If it be claimed that the point of the remark 'He is turning it into a merely conceptual dispute' is simply to say that he is not *going* to back down in the light of *anything* else that may happen, then the remark is a simple, though possibly justified, accusation of irrationality. If it doesn't sound accusatory to the casual ear, then so much the worse (PQ might add) for the effects on the casual ear of bad theories of confirmation and of the ASD.

(2) An elucidatory and anti-Quinean power is often claimed for such locutions as this: 'The world can't make me wrong about that, whereas with this other it is always *possible* that something will happen which will make me withdraw it.' But PQ can reply: 'The first half of what you have just said is true only if you fail to take into account certain sorts of possibility of falsification, namely, all the possibilities the simplest accommodations of which would involve the denial of highly indispensable sentences now called analytic. *Of course* there is a bump in the scale if you cut part of it off; but if you take the whole situation into account, the continuity is still there. And if your remarks of the form "I can't be shown wrong about *that*" refer not to sentences but to the propositions they express, then you have indeed established a discontinuity between "analytic" and "synthetic" when these words are applied to propositions; but this is of no interest, since the "proposition" terminology itself is built

3. An accommodation of all the facts known to X is a totality of accepted sentences with respect to which none of X's experiences is recalcitrant.

out of the "sentence" terminology (in my theory, anyway, and I am still waiting to be shown that it is wrong) in such a way that propositional identity shades smoothly into propositional non-identity; so that the discontinuity which you seem to have established is illusory.'

This line of argument invites the hostile question 'Are you saying that until we know whether later developments are going to lead us to withdraw an analytic sentence, we can't be confident that it is true *now*?' This question's hostility derives from its tacit assumption of the distinction, mentioned earlier, between 'was true, is false' and 'was false all along, though accepted.' There are countless ways in which this distinction can insinuate itself into the debate, but perhaps this one should be dealt with, for its own sake and as an example of the way in which, it seems, we must handle 'true' if we wish to beg no questions about intensional terminology. What PQ must say is that, if $S$ is accepted at $t_1$ and rejected at $t_2$, the way to settle at $t_2$ whether $S$ was false at $t_1$ is to find out whether its rejection came about as part of an over-all adjustment which included the rejection of sentences which were at $t_1$ indispensable enough to warrant the label 'analytic.' If $S$ was rejected without going as deep as the rejection of anything analytic, then it is proper to describe $S$ as having been false, though accepted; but if its rejection was, or was accompanied by, the rejection of an analytic sentence, then there is no reason at $t_2$ for saying that $S$ was false at $t_1$.[4] The upshot of this is that to be false is to be due for what we might call superficial rejection; and it follows that if a sentence is analytic at $t_1$ it will never be proper to say that it was false at $t_1$; if it is synthetic at $t_1$ it may become proper to say that it was false at $t_1$; both of which are just the results we should expect if PQ's theory is to be viable at all.

(3) 'I base my acceptance of that simply on my knowledge of the use of words, but no one is rationally entitled to accept this other just on such a slim basis as the use of words.' To this PQ can reply: 'The trouble with that sort of talk is that it draws the line you wish to draw only by construing the phrase "use of

---

4. For strict accuracy, the phrase 'accompanied by' needs careful qualification. *Cf.* footnote 2 *supra.*

words" in a highly special way. Is it a fact about how words are used that the word "non-human" applies to everything to which the phrase "born in Antarctica" applies? You will have to say "No"; and if the enquirer into the meaning of intensional terminology then asks you what you *do* count as being "about the use of words," you will presumably have to follow all the others who have travelled this route and refer him to rules of *meaning* or something of the sort. You cannot avoid the use of "meaning" by appealing to dictionaries: they give all sorts of information which you wouldn't want to regard as analytic; and if you appeal not to dictionaries as they sit there on the shelf, but to dictionaries considered as fulfilling the characteristic lexicographic function, then we are back at "meaning" again. So your appeal to "use of words" seems to be just another *instance* of what I am saying in my negative thesis. And if your original pair of remarks is appropriately amended by substituting "meanings" for "use," it becomes manifestly harmless to my positive thesis.'

(4) 'If you denied that, I shouldn't have any idea of what you were getting at—I should be simply bewildered—but if you denied this other, I should be surprised but I should know what to expect.' PQ can reply: 'That is true only because of the way you have selected your cases. If you take some sentence which we both regard as synthetic and which we both have, and know each other to have, powerful reasons for regarding as true and none worth mentioning for regarding as false; and if I then deny that sentence; you will be just as bewildered as you would be if I said that I had drawn a square circle. If I say "It will rain this afternoon" you will take an umbrella; if I say "It will both rain and be fine all afternoon" you won't know what to do—agreed; but if, as we look out of the window at the sunshine, I say "It is raining so hard that you shouldn't go out," which of the other two situations is this more like?'

This fourth example is the one given by Grice and Strawson, and I am indebted to Mr. Grice for, amongst much else, some comments on my treatment of it. He grants that 'It is raining so hard that you shouldn't go out' may be bewildering *in some circumstances,* but says that it is not *prima facie* bewildering as is 'It will both rain and be fine all afternoon.' But what does *prima facie* mean here? The only relevant sense I can attach to it is 'bewildering whatever one does or does not happen to know about the world,' and even this is relevant only if one excludes that set of facts to which adherents of the traditional ASD constantly appeal—the behavioral facts determining what is to be said about meanings. If this set of facts can be located in a non-question-begging way, then we can save example (4), or even bypass it and perform the more useful task of saving example (3). But *can* it be located in the way required? The fact that Grice and Strawson select an approach through bewilderingness suggests, perhaps misleadingly, that they are pessimistic about the chances of making a successful frontal attack on 'meaning'; such a pessimism would certainly be justified by the literature.[5] In brief, then, it seems that the difference-in-kind alleged in example (4) to constitute a partial elucidation of the ASD has to be understood in terms of the notion of a sentence's being bewildering to anyone who knows the *meanings* of its constituent terms even if that is all he knows. Indeed, this fact is explicitly recognized by Grice and Strawson when they say, rightly, that the denial of an analytic sentence will be bewildering only if one assumes that the words involved are not being used in 'a figurative or unusual sense.' This is a use of intensional terminology in defense of 'Denials of analytic sentences are bewildering' which is exactly parallel to the use of intensional terminology which I have just tried to show to be necessary in defense of 'Denials of synthetic sentences are not bewildering.' In each case it seems that the explanation of intensional terminology—granted that it is intended to be only partial and (perhaps) approximate—cannot be given *at all* without the use of intensional terminology. In the light of all this, it is not clear to me what Grice and Strawson wish to claim when they say that their explanation 'breaks out of the family-circle.'

---

5. I allude here mainly to the long history of evasion of the problem, particularly of the problem as set by Quine's powerful statement of the difficulties in "The Problem of Meaning in Linguistics" (ch. III of *From a Logical Point of View*).

## 4. A NON-QUINEAN THEORY OF THE ASD

A rough account of what is to be attempted in this section may be given as follows: Instead of taking the statement that some sentences are traditionally analytic (i.e., in a sense such that the Quinean analysis is not adequate) in every confirmation-situation and then forlornly trying to qualify it, putting 'proposition' for 'sentence' and the like, in such a way as to make it true, I shall make an independent attempt to establish the weaker statement that in every confirmation-situation some sentence (meaning *sentence*) is traditionally analytic. Just what this means should emerge in the course of the argument.

As a starting point, let us consider a story of the sort told in illustration of Quine's thesis that no sentence undergoes, solo, confirmation or disconfirmation at the hands of any experience. For example: We find in Australia those birds which in fact led people to say that there are black swans; and the finding of them is a recalcitrant experience, in the sense that now that this has happened *something* of what we have been accustomed to saying must be denied. In this particular case, easily the best thing to sacrifice is 'All swans are white' and a few others; but we could save this and instead sacrifice 'Birds which are thus and so are swans' together with a good deal of our taxonomy and the natural history depending on it; or we could save all that too, and sacrifice instead 'Nothing is black all over and white all over' together with very large stretches of talk which depend upon certain features of our use of color-terminology; or . . . etc., etc. There are many intermediate possibilities, such as the introduction of geographical qualifications into the laws of optics, and an acceptance of consequent revisions of physics and neurophysiology; and no remark about the consequences of any particular sacrifice is absolute: we can drive a wedge between any sentence and any other sentence so long as we are prepared to pay an appropriate price.

It is of first importance to notice that this pattern of disconfirmation does not ever allow us to say 'Well, if I *can* save S, then I *shall* save it and there's an end of the matter': the end of the matter always comes just after a sacrifice, not just after a save. If this were not so, there would be no such thing as recalcitrance.

A question which can be raised after the saving of any sentence—say of $S_1$—is 'Why must I make some other sacrifice?' The answer must be of the form 'Because the set of sentences you now accept is inconsistent with the occurrence of the experience $E$'; but Quine must give this answer in the special form 'Because you accept sentence $S_2$ which compels you, now that $E$ has occurred, to sacrifice $S_1$.' One could save $S_2$ as well, but then some other sacrifice must be made, 'Because you accept $S_3$ which compels you, now that $E$ has occurred, to reject either $S_1$ or $S_2$.' Now, the trouble with this is that Quine must refuse to allow the process to come to an end. For the only way in which he can call a halt at, say the $n$th step is to answer the $n$th asking of 'Why must I make some other sacrifice?' with 'Because it just *is* the case, whatever else you may be given to saying, that in the light of experience $E$ you cannot retain the conjunction $S_1.S_2 \ldots S_n$'; and this would be tantamount to admitting that there is a sentence (albeit a long one) which is, in isolation, strongly disconfirmed by an experience.

There is no logical objection to this infinite regress. The most likely form for it to take would be for members of a small group of logical laws to appear repeatedly, first 'neat,' then in instances of ever-increasing length, each instance being formed by the substitution *of* laws which have already occurred in the regress *in* laws which have already occurred in the regress. This could go on for as long as one liked, without its becoming simply repetitious.

But although the question 'Why must some other sacrifice be made?' can always be answered without repetition—that is, without appealing to any member of the group of sentences whose joint saving is in question—it is not at all clear that it can always be answered also with truth. Certainly, it is true for only a finite number of distinct values of $s$ that $s$ is in a literal sense a sentence which Smith calls true: Smith has considered at most a few million sentences, many of those he calls false, and of the rest only a few dozen are likely to be relevant in a given confirmation-situation. So we must look for some sense in which we can say that each sacrifice is forced upon Smith by a sentence which he already regards as true, without our having to admit that the relevant sentence has in fact ever been explicitly considered by Smith.

It might seem possible to avoid the difficulty by construing 'Smith calls S true' at least sometimes as 'Smith calls true something which leads by logic to S,' thus making it possible for Smith to call true an infinity of sentences, gathered into bundles each of which consists of the logical consequences of some sentence which Smith *explicitly* calls true. But this device does not solve the problem, for the conditions under which something 'follows by logic' from something else are precisely what the Quinean theory is about anyway. Whether we give the center of our attention to the possibility of gathering sentences into bundles, or to the more general problem of sacrifices and saves, it remains true wherever Quine says that one sentence follows by logic from another he must allow each step in the 'following from' to be the locus of a possible sacrifice of something called true. Therefore, no attempt of this sort to tie 'sentences called true' into bundles can effect any reduction in the number of sentences *explicitly* called true, for (to put it another way) in each bundle there can be no more member-sentences than there are sentences holding the bundle together, and each of the latter sentences must be either explicitly called true or be a member of a further bundle which is held together by further sentences each of which is either . . . and so on, *ad infinitum*.

Consider Achilles and the Tortoise in Lewis Carroll's story. Their trouble had its origin in the Tortoise's refusal to allow any sort of move from premise to conclusion—his tacit departure from the usual convention whereby any move from antecedent to consequent of an analytic conditional is deemed legitimate, without replacing this convention by either a more or a less liberal one. The result of this is, so to speak, a refusal to treat anything as analytic: every step must be explicitly justified before it can be taken and, since *justifying* is itself *taking a step*, this means that no step can be taken at all.

This relates closely to the difficulty confronting Quine. Although his stress is not upon the alleged need explicitly to justify each step in an argument but rather on the alleged possibility of making any step illegitimate by the taking of appropriate avoiding action, the former implies the latter and therefore shares its difficulties: for the only way in which it can be the case (as Quine seems committed to saying it is) that any logical move from one sentence to another can be avoided by the denial of some other sentence the assertion of which is necessary for the legitimacy of the move, is for it to be the case (as the Tortoise pretends it is) that for any logical move from one sentence to another there is some sentence the assertion of which is necessary for the legitimacy of the move.[6]

Another suggestion for the required sense of 'calls true' is simply that of 'is disposed to call true,' which would solve the problem of finitude at once. Following out the consequences of this suggestion: Smith registers $E$'s recalcitrance; decides (perhaps) to retain every relevant sentence he has ever formulated; but then—being honest and energetic—casts around to formulate and then reject some sentence which he has never explicitly considered before but which has the following two properties: (i) If it *had* been put to him before $E$ occurred he *would* have called it true (and thus it is, in the sense of this paper, a sentence which was until $E$'s occurrence a member of the set of sentences 'accepted by' Smith); (ii) Formulation and rejection of it provides an accommodation of $E$—that is, modifies Smith's set of accepted sentences in such a way that $E$ is no longer recalcitrant with respect to it.

Suppose, though, that Smith's energy is not equal to his honesty, and that his reaction to the recalcitrant experience goes like this instead: he decides to retain every relevant sentence he has ever formulated; he acknowledges that there must be some sentence which he has never thought about but (a) which he would in the past have called true if it had been put to him, and (b) which he must not in future call true if he does ever

6. Here too I am indebted to Quine. See his "Truth by Convention" in O. H. Lee, ed., *Philosophical Essays for A. N. Whitehead* (New York, 1936), where considerations of this sort are argued with force and clarity against logical conventionalism but not, of course, against Quine's current position which he did not at that time hold.

confront it in an explicit form; he decides not to go hunting for it now but to forget the whole matter until such a sentence does turn up; but even then he does not guarantee to reject the *first* such sentence to turn up. Can he not claim that by thus disposing himself to recognize and reject some such sentence he is, *a fortiori*, disposing himself to reject some such sentence? And is not this all that is required for him to have effected an accommodation of *E*? It is clear that if this pattern of 'accommodation' is followed often enough, we shall begin to question Smith's honesty: it will before long be fair to say 'He doesn't back down on *anything:* he keeps saying that he *could* straighten it all out by means of [no doubt] a conceptual revision, but he never produces the conceptual revision.' But, while it seems clear that this would be a legitimate charge, it is not easy to see why it should be so if the original suggestion—that the recalcitrance-producing pressure could come from a sentence Smith has been disposed to call true but has never formulated—is correct. For if we combine the Quinean claim that whatever sentences we retain in the face of *E* there is always some remaining way of accommodating *E*, with the current proposal that recalcitrance may be created by a combination of sentences-thought-of-but-still-retained with sentences-still-unformulated, there seems to be no reason at all why the ever-possible saving adjustments in face of *E* should not remain in the latter category of sentences-still-unformulated.

Someone who combines these two views is, of course, entitled to a natural suspicion of Smith's forever unsubstantiated claims to be able in practice to carry out the required formulations and rejections; but there is no reason why Smith should make such claims in the first place. On the view I am now considering, there is no reason why Smith should not admit that *he* cannot *show* that it is all right for him to say the things that he does say, and simply adduce general Quinean theory as his reason for saying that nevertheless there must always *be* some way in which this *could* be shown. In brief: We have here two kinds of generosity—Quine's about our freedom of choice in making adjustments, and the other about our right to keep silent—which *together* produce the result that there is nothing theoretically wrong with refusing to let experience modify anything we actually say.

I conclude that neither the 'follows by logic' nor the 'disposed to call true' approaches will solve the difficulty with which this section has been concerned; and the apparent absence of any viable alternative solution leads to the conclusion that in any experiential situation, if the experiences involved are to offer a challenge to *any* sentences then there must be some sentences to which they offer no challenge at all—some sentences which simply are not up for possible revision in the particular situation concerned. This is what was meant by the declaration with which this section began: in every confirmation-situation, some sentence is traditionally analytic.

It may look as though this claim is weak not only in respect of its placing of the crucial quantifier, but also in respect of the way in which that quantifier is to be understood; that is, it might be suggested that the *only* force of saying that in any confirmation-situation there are sentences which are not up for revision is simply to deny that there are no such sentences, not to suggest any way in which we could sometimes *find* one. But although the arguments so far used have been of the form 'There are such sentences, because we cannot allow that there are not,' more can be said than this. I have come to it by a route through the enemy's camp—through general objections to Quinean theory rather than by the positive development of a contrary theory—primarily because the statement that there are sentences of this sort can be argued for without providing a way for finding any, relative merely to confirmation-*situations;* while to be able to say of a given sentence that *it* is of the required sort we must be able to relate it not just to a confirmation-situation but to an individual person propounding an *argument* about that situation.

A constructive account of 'analytic in the argument' must proceed through an account of 'involved in the argument.' To discover what sentences are involved in the argument whereby Smith concludes 'Because $E$ has occurred, $S_1$ is true,' we must ask Smith, for there is always a choice of routes for any given experience-sentence pair. How does Smith decide that, say, $S_2$

is involved in his argument? Surely, by seeing that his reason for saying 'If $E$ has occurred, $S_1$ is true' is that he accepts as true both $S_2$ and 'If $S_2$ is true then if $E$ has occurred then $S_1$ is true'; and he accepts this last as true because he accepts both $S_3$ and 'If $S_3$ is true then if $S_2$ is true, then . . .'; and so on backwards, but not *ad infinitum*. For at some stage he will say something like 'I accept $S_n$ as true and $S_n$ *says that* if $S_{o-1}$ is true then . . .' The phrase 'says that' does not matter; what *is* important is Smith's arrival at a stopping-place (or at stopping-places; but for brevity I shall deal only with cases where the 'involvement' sequence does not ramify) at which he says 'There is nothing more to say. Accepting $S_n$ is accepting . . . , and not through the mediation of anything else, either.'

The terminal sentence in the 'involvement' sequence could be said to be analytic in that argument. Normally it will not be stated in the argument, but if it is stated it will be labelled as a rule of inference or in some other way which would make it clear that no further-back sentences are admitted by Smith to be in need of statement at all in this argument. As a rule, Smith will choose the terminus which most people would choose in such an argument, because as a rule he will wish to use words in their normal senses and not propose any conceptual revisions. This way of putting things presupposes—what I should wish to defend—a definition of 'analytic' as 'analytic in most arguments,' and a consequent development of the rest of the standard intensional terminology on this basis.

A sentence may fall short of Smith's terminus and still not be considered by him as on the cards for possible revision; but his terminal sentence and all that lies behind it are *put* off the cards for possible revision by the very shape of Smith's argument—that is, by his insistence that once he has worked back to $S_n$ *there is* nothing more to say—and it is with *impossibility* of revision that I am here concerned. Of course, $S_n$ might be considered for revision, or at least located short of the terminus, in another argument; but sensible criteria for the identity of arguments would demand that it be considered *another* argument. I grant that this is an elementary definitional matter, but it is not a definitional matter that this definition has application.

It can be cashed only because we have a straightforwardly empirical sense for the notion of a *complete argument* (and a set of logical considerations to confute those who take the line that the appearance of completeness is always misleading and that no actually occurring argument is really complete in the required sense), and this gives us a straightforwardly empirical sense for the notion of argument non-identity. Contrast this with what happens when PQ's theory is applied to standard remarks about 'different meaning,' 'different use,' 'different proposition,' and the rest.

The conclusions so far reached in this section have a certain tameness, stemming particularly from the fact that the identification of any given sentence as analytic in a given argument may well lack the confidence of the claim that *some* sentence must be analytic in the argument. But there are lessons to be learned from the development of a doctrine of analyticity in this way. For brevity, I shall state them in an assured and unqualified fashion which may well not be warranted by the arguments which I have presented.

The situation is this: Quine claims that sentences are never used in the way in which his critics say that analytic sentences are used, namely, in such a way that they are not capable of revision in the light of the facts. The standard reply to this is that there are two sorts of revision, conceptual and factual, a claim which (as the device of PQ has been used to show) cannot in any obvious way be made good. The upshot of the arguments advanced in the present paper is that Quine is wrong—that there is, and indeed must be, an analytic use of sentences in a traditional sense of 'analytic'—but that Quine's critics, while underestimating the force of his arguments and the strength of his position, have granted him too much. In particular, they have apparently granted him that any sentence is at all times capable of revision of one sort or the other; and this has put them in the position of having to establish an important difference of kind between the situation where an analytic sentence is denied and that in which a synthetic sentence is denied. On the basis of the arguments I have offered, all that is required is the establishment of an important difference of kind between the argument in which a sentence is up for possible revision of some sort and the argument in which it cannot be up for revision *at all*. If the arguments of this section are in order, the difference between the two arguments is absolute—it is, for instance, not capable of analysis in PQ's way—and if Quine or PQ should object that sensible people never treat sentences in such a way as to rule out the question of their possible falsification, we are in a position to reply that sensible people must sometimes treat sentences in this way if they are to be capable of constructing arguments at all.

Note added in 1969: I stand by the first three sections. The fourth raises a genuine difficulty for the Quinean position, but I now think it can be met in Quinean terms. Even if it cannot, my own attempt to parlay it into a defense of the traditional account of the ASD is an embarrassing failure.

# ON 'ANALYTIC'

## R. M. Martin

*Several writers have replied to the antagonists of the analytic-synthetic distinction that their demands are exorbitant. R. M. Martin replies in such a manner in "On 'Analytic.'" Quine wants a definition of 'S is analytic in L' for all S and for all L, but Martin questions whether any sense can really be made of this relation for all S and all L. To demand a notion of analyticity which would be suitable for both formalized and natural languages is unreasonable. One can imagine the kind of questions which Martin has in mind: "What kind of variables do natural languages contain? Are they finite or transfinite? Do all natural languages contain variables of the same kind? What is the basic structure of natural languages—Russell's theory of types of Zermelo's axiomatic set theory? Are natural languages consistent*

From *Philosophical Studies*, vol. 3, 1952. Reprinted by permission of *Philosophical Studies* and the author.

*or inconsistent?" Such questions regarding natural languages seem hopeless, yet to ignore them is to abandon the precision and care "which Frege, Carnap, and Tarski have taught us."*

*To demand even a general definition for all formalized languages is asking too much. Martin points out that such "general" definitions are not available for the notions of truth and derivability.*

*Quine's objection to the use of semantical rules is really based on a misunderstanding, according to Martin, because Carnap is quite clear about what semantical rules are. In the case of specific languages, they are definitions in the metalanguage; and in general semantics, they are semantical axioms in the metalanguage. Interpreted in either way, Martin thinks that Carnap was right about the indispensability of such rules for doing semantics, and Quine's objections against such rules can only be taken as objections to doing what he is demanding otherwise.*

*One wonders whether the objections raised by Quine and White can be put off legitimately so easily. Could the amount of attention given to the problems raised by these men and the numerous serious responses made by reputable philosophers be taken as evidence that the demands being made are reasonable after all?*

Quine and, in his wake, White have recently urged that we have no clear-cut, "fundamental," or "sharp" distinction between analytic and synthetic truths.[1] Analytic truths are commonly regarded as statements depending for their truths on meanings and not on matters of fact, whereas synthetic statements depend for their truth upon matters of fact in a quite basic way. Quine regards the distinction as an "ill-founded dogma" of recent em-

---

1. See W. V. Quine, "Two Dogmas of Empiricism," *Philosophical Review*, 60 (1951): 20–43, and M. G. White, "The Analytic and the Synthetic: An Untenable Dualism," in *John Dewey: Philosopher of Science and Freedom*, ed. by S. Hook (New York: Dial Press, 1950), pp. 316–30. For a summary and an interesting discussion of these papers, see Benson Mates, "Analytic Sentences," *Philosophical Review*, 60 (1951): 525–34.

piricism, and urges either that we abandon it altogether or "at best" make it a distinction of "degree" not of "kind." White echoes this view, seeing in the distinction a "myth" and an "untenable dualism."

No one has drawn the distinction between 'analytic' (*L*-true) and 'synthetic' (factual) more clearly or with greater care and precision than Carnap.[2] Therefore it might seem that it is primarily certain of Carnap's writings that are under attack. At only two or three points, however, in the papers of Quine and White, is Carnap's way of drawing the distinction discussed in detail. In the main body of these papers it seems to be rather certain philosophers of "natural" language who are supposed to bear the brunt of the attack. However this may be, it is the purpose of the present note not so much to defend Carnap's distinction as to show that neither Quine nor White has said anything really substantial against it.

Everyone seems to agree that if 'analytic' and 'synthetic' are to be discussed clearly, it must be done relative to a language. Thus we are not concerned with 'analytic' so much as with 'analytic in *L*,' where *L* stands for a language system. The first matter we might reasonably inquire into is the character of the language systems *L* being considered.

Carnap is always explicit about the character of the language systems he discusses. To be explicit in this way would seem to be a *sine qua non* of all clear philosophical discourse about language. The language systems Carnaps deals with, in his recent writings, are of the kind techincally known as simple, applied, logical calculi of first order.[3] The syntactical structure of these language systems is well known. All of Carnap's recent discussions of 'analytic' or '*L-true*' are concerned only with well-founded language systems of this kind.

Quine wishes to discuss the problem of gaining a clear defini-

2. See *Meaning and Necessity* (Chicago: University of Chicago Press, 1947) and *The Logical Foundations of Probability* (Chicago: University of Chicago Press, 1950), Chap. III.

3. See A. Church, *Introduction to Mathematical Logic* (Princeton: Princeton University Press, 1944), p. 37.

tion of 'analytic' in more general terms. He wishes to discuss
the term 'analytic in $L$' for variable '$L$,' '$L$' ranging over *all*
languages. To demand a definition of 'analytic in $L$,' where '$L$'
is taken as ranging over just the thoroughly studied *formalized*
languages, is to make what at present would seem to be an
exorbitant demand. Quine asks for not only this but more. He
wishes a definition of 'analytic in $L$' where '$L$' ranges over the
*natural* languages also. To demand this is to demand *much*
more than seems reasonable on the basis of present knowledge.
Why not ask the same concerning the semantical *truth* concept
or of the syntactical *derivability* relation? The semantical truth
concept, for example, has been defined precisely only as applied
to certain kinds of formalized language systems. No one has put
forward a definition of 'true in $L$' where '$L$' ranges over the
natural languages. Nor have the other concepts of syntax and
semantics been defined in such great generality. To demand *con
fuoco* such generality of a definition of 'analytic in $L$' and not of
the other concepts of syntax and semantics seems curious indeed.

All talk of the logical structure of natural language, if careful
and precise, is fraught with difficulties. The most elementary
questions one wishes to ask here seem to resist definitive answers. What kinds of variables does natural language contain?
Does it contain variables of only finite order, in the sense of
simplified type theory, or does it also contain some variables of
transfinite level? What is the structure of the logic underlying
natural language? Is it a type theory, or is it more akin to the
Zermelo axiomatic set theory? And so on.

Also, because of the presence of the logical as well as of the
semantical or epistemological antinomies, it seems very likely
that natural language, even just its declarative, cognitive part, is
inconsistent.[4] For consistent $L$, the term 'analytic in $L$' seems
scarcely worth bothering about. For inconsistent $L$, presumably
*every* sentence of $L$ is analytic. To talk about natural $L$, with the
kind of care and precision necessary for clear-minded philosophy,
without indicating how one would give an explicit, consistent

---

4. See A. Tarski, "Der Wahrheitsbegriff in den formalisierten Sprachen,"
*Studia Philosophica*, 1 (1936): 261–405, esp. pp. 267–79.

formalization of it, is to forget the very first lessons which Frege, Carnap, and Tarski have taught us!

But even where we restrict our discussion to formalized language systems, Quine insists that "the problem is to make sense of this relation (the relation between statement S and languages L of being an analytic statement of) generally, that is, for variable 'S' and variable 'L.'" He goes on, "The point that I wish to make is that the gravity of this problem is not perceptibly less for artificial languages than for natural ones." But if Tarski's argument concerning the inconsistency of natural languages is sound, then the two problems here are indeed different!

Quine goes on, "The problem of making sense of the idiom 'S is analytic for L' . . . retains its stubbornness even if we limit the range of the variable 'L' to artificial languages." [5] Indeed, one agrees with this statement. But the problem of making sense of the idiom 'S is *true* in L,' for variable 'S' and for 'L' ranging over all formalized languages, also retains its stubbornness, and in fact is unsolved. Tarski's method of truth definition, in *Der Wahrheitsbegriff*, for example, is inapplicable to systems based upon simplified type theory or upon the Zermelo set theory (unless transfinite types are allowed in the metalanguage). And when the truth definitions for such languages are given, the methods are sufficiently different from those used for defining 'truth' as applied to weaker language systems that it is by no means clear that both kinds of definition are mere instances of a general definition of 'S is true in L,' for variable 'S' and variable 'L.'

At present we have no truth concept of the immense generality Quine demands of the concept of analytic. Similar remarks hold concerning many of the basic concepts of syntax as well. To demand *ab initio* a definition of these concepts applying to all formalized language systems uniformly, seems to be a violation of sound methodology. The best we can hope to do at the present stage of research is to do as Carnap has done, to confine attention exclusively to languages having a very simple

5. Quine, "Two Dogmas of Empiricism," pp. 31–32.

structure. The hope is, of course, that our definitions can then be extended to languages of greater complexity. But whether this can be done successfully is a matter for future research.

Both Quine and White seem to have had difficulties understanding what *Semantical Rules* are. Quine states that "the relative term 'semantical rule of' is as much in need of clarification, at least, as 'analytic for,'" and that "Semantical rules are distinguishable, apparently, only by the fact of appearing on a page under the heading 'Semantical Rules'. . . ." [6] Now it seems fairly evident that, in Carnap's formulations of semantics, semantical rules are to be regarded either as (1) definitions in the metalanguage, or as (2) semantical axioms in the metalanguage.

In *specific* semantics, where we are dealing exclusively with the semantics of a particular language system $L_0$, the semantical rules are usually regarded by Carnap as definitions. Here, where one employs a metalanguage containing variables and quantifiers over objects of higher logical types than those contained in $L_0$, the semantical rules define for us such terms as 'true in $L_0$,' 'satisfies in $L_0$,' 'designates in $L_0$,' etc. In *general* semantics, where we discuss several object languages comparatively and where one or more semantical concepts are needed as metalinguistic primitives, the semantical rules may figure as both definitions and axioms. Some of them may be axioms characterizing the semantical primitives, and the others, definitions of further semantical concepts in terms of the primitives.

Thus in either case, we know quite well what the semantical rules are. To object to them in the sense (1) is to object to semantical truth definitions of the Tarski kind. And to object to them in the sense (2) would seem tantamount to objecting to the very kind of *general* semantics Quine is apparently demanding! Any formulation of a theory of general semantics in terms of special semantical primitives must contain, it would seem, some semantical rules in the sense of axioms. Construed in either way, semantical rules are an obviously necessary part of the formal apparatus of semantics, because axioms or rules and (in practice) definitions are necessary for the construction of any

6. *Ibid.*, p. 33, and White, "The Analytic and the Synthetic," pp. 321–22.

formalized language. It is as idle and pointless to state that semantical rules are known as such only by appearing on a page under a certain heading as to say the same, *mutatis mutandis*, of the axioms and definitions of a formalized arithmetic!

It is also important to note that Carnap intends his distinction as an *explication* of some age-old concepts. By an explication Carnap understands the task of making more exact, clear, and precise an older, less clear, less precise concept, usually of historical importance. The vague concept "may belong to everyday language or to a previous stage in the development of scientific language," whereas the more exact concept "must be given by explicit rules for its use, for example, by a definition which incorporates it into a well-constructed system of scientific either logicomathematical or empirical concepts." [7]

The definition of '*L*-true' is intended as an explication of the older notion of necessary or analytic truth. Whatever the ultimate destiny of Carnap's definitions of the *L*-concepts may turn out to be, there can be little doubt that they do provide an explication in the sense described of several historically important concepts. In the case of 'analytic,' the use of this word or of '*L*-true' or 'logically true' for the new, more exact concept is merely suggestive. One could as well call it '$K_0$' or whatever. It is only the new concept that is being rigorously defined. That the new concept is an explication for the older concept is indicated by using the same word for both.

Quine would allow us to write "untendentiously" some noncommittal expression, say '*K*,' in place of 'analytic in *L*,' "so as not to seem to throw light on the interesting word 'analytic.'" But this is to miss the point that Carnap's definition aims to explicate the older concept of logical or necessary truth. Similar remarks apply equally well to the semantical truth concept. We could call the precise term 'frue,' as Tarski suggests somewhere, rather than 'true,' so as not to seem to throw light on the age-old, hoary concept of truth. But this would be to miss the point of the explicative power of the new definition.

Finally, there is the matter of the fruitfulness of Carnap's

7. Carnap, *Logical Foundations of Probability*, p. 3.

distinction for science and methodology. For a distinction to be "fundamental" in some metaphysical or intuitive sense would seem less important than for it to be methodologically or heuristically useful. On the basis of the L-concepts Carnap has given (1) an exact and careful analysis of the concepts of modality, and (2) the foundations of a systematic theory of degree of confirmation or of inductive logic. Now Quine is clearly no lover of modalities. Many feel, however, that the modal concepts will prove to be of genuine importance for the methodology of the sciences. Several kinds of questions in the logical analysis of science seem to involve the L-concepts in one way or another, for example, questions concerning the exhaustiveness of a set of competitive theories, or concerning the incompatibility of theories or of laws within the same theory. For a logical analysis of so unsuspected a field as that of the economic theory of marketing, one expert (a friend of the writer) thinks the modal concepts essential. One simply cannot say in advance what their importance will prove to be.

That the L-concepts are needed for Carnap's recent work on the logic of confirmation is relevant also. It is very difficult to see how a concept of degree of confirmation could be constructed, along Carnap's lines at least, without the notion of L-falsity.[8] It is not being urged that the L-concepts are to be judged *solely* on the grounds of their "cash value" for science and methodology, but only that this must be taken into account. Quine and White never mention these important applications of the L-concepts, as though they were quite irrelevant.

To summarize, the following points have been made: (1) We must be clear about the logical character of the object language with respect to which the concepts of analytic and synthetic are to be distinguished. (2) Quine's demand for a definition of 'analytic in L' for 'L' ranging over the *natural* languages is exorbitant. (3) The demand for a definition of 'analytic in L' for 'L' ranging over all *formalized* language systems *ab initio* is at best premature. (4) Quine's difficulties concerning semantical rules

8. See *ibid.*, pp. 289, 295, and *passim*.

seem to be based on misunderstandings. (5) Carnap's definitions of the *L*-concepts are intended as explicata for an important nexus of age-old concepts. (6) The *L*-concepts may prove to be helpful in the logical analysis of science.

Carnap's Principle of Tolerance in Syntax (and Semantics) needs reaffirmation!

# SELECTED BIBLIOGRAPHY

## BOOKS

R. Ammerman, *Classics of Analytic Philosophy*, New York: McGraw-Hill Book Co., 1965.

A. J. Ayer, *Language, Truth, and Logic*, London: Gollancz, 1936, 1946.

P. Bennaceraf and H. Putnam, *Philosophy of Mathematics*, Englewood Cliffs: Prentice-Hall, Inc., 1964.

G. Bergmann, *Meaning and Existence*, Madison: University of Wisconsin Press, 1959.

M. Black, *Language and Philosophy*, Ithaca, New York: Cornell University Press, 1949.

————, *Problems of Analysis*, Ithaca, New York: Cornell University Press, 1954.

M. Bunge, *Metascientific Queries*, Springfield, Illinois: Charles C. Thomas, Publishers, 1959.

————, *The Myth of Simplicity*, Englewood Cliffs: Prentice-Hall, Inc., 1963.

R. Carnap, *The Logical Syntax of Language*, New York: Harcourt Brace, 1937.

————, *Introduction to Semantics,* Cambridge: Harvard University Press, 1942.

————, *Meaning and Necessity,* Chicago: The University of Chicago Press, 1947 and 1956.

H. W. Cassirer, *Kant's First Critique,* New York: The Macmillan Co., 1954.

H. Feigl and W. Sellars, *Readings in Philosophical Analysis,* New York: Appleton-Century-Crofts, 1949.

———— and M. Scriven, *Minnesota Studies in the Philosophy of Science,* 3 vols., Minneapolis: University of Minnesota Press, 1956.

———— and G. Maxwell, *Current Issues in the Philosophy of Science,* New York: Holt, Rinehart, and Winston, 1961.

F. B. Fitch, *Symbolic Logic,* New York: Ronald Press, 1952.

A. G. N. Flew, *Logic and Language, First Series,* Oxford: Blackwell, 1952.

————, *Logic and Language, Second Series,* Oxford: Blackwell, 1961.

C. Hartshorne, *The Logic of Perfection and Other Essays in Neoclassical Metaphysics,* LaSalle, Illinois: Open Court Publishing Co., 1962.

S. Hook, *American Philosophers at Work,* New York: Criterion Books, 1956.

B. Kazemier and D. Vuyaje, *Logic and Language,* Dordrecht-Holland: D. Reidel Publishing Co., 1963.

L. Linsky, *Semantics and the Philosophy of Language,* Urbana: University of Illinois Press, 1952.

R. Martin, *The Notion of Analytic Truth,* Philadelphia: University of Pennsylvania Press, 1959.

E. Nagel, *Logic without Metaphysics,* Glencoe, Illinois: The Free Press, 1956.

A. Pap, *Elements of Analytic Philosophy,* New York: The Macmillan Co., 1949.

————, *Semantics and Necessary Truth,* New Haven: Yale University Press, 1958.

K. Popper, *Conjectures and Refutations,* New York: Basic Books, 1962.

W. Quine, *Mathematical Logic,* Cambridge: Harvard University Press, rev. ed., 1951.

————, *From a Logical Point of View,* New York: Harper and Row, Publishers, 1953.

————, *Methods of Logic,* New York: Holt, Rinehart, and Winston, rev. ed., 1959.

————, *Word and Object,* New York and London: The Technology

Press of the Massachusetts Institute of Technology and John Wiley and Sons, Inc., 1960.

H. Reichenbach, *The Rise of Scientific Philosophy*, Berkeley: University of California Press, 1951.

R. Robinson, *Definition*, Oxford at the Clarendon Press, 1950.

B. Russell, *Problems of Philosophy*, Oxford: Oxford University Press, 1912.

————, *Introduction to Mathematical Philosophy*, New York and London: The Humanities Press, 1919.

————, *An Inquiry into Meaning and Truth*, New York: Norton Publishers, 1940.

P. A. Schilpp, *The Philosophy of Rudolf Carnap*, LaSalle, Illinois: Open Court Publishing Co., 1963.

A. Tarski, *Logic, Semantics, Metamathematics*, Oxford at the Clarendon Press, 1956.

M. White, *Toward Reunion in Philosophy*, Cambridge: Harvard University Press, 1956.

L. Wittgenstein, *Tractatus Logico Philosophicus*, New York: The Humanities Press, 1961.

————, *Remarks on the Foundations of Mathematics*, New York: The Macmillan Co., 1956.

A. N. Whitehead and B. Russell, *Principia Mathematica*, 3 vols., Cambridge: Cambridge University Press, 1910–1913. 2nd ed., 1925–1927.


ARTICLES


P. Achinstein, "Defeasible Problems," *Journal of Philosophy*, 62 (1965).

K. Ajdukiewicz, "Le problème du fondement des propositions analytiques," *Studia Logica*, 8 (1959).

————, "On Syntactical Coherence"; tr. P. T. Geach, *Review of Metaphysics*, 20 (1967).

A. Ambrose, "Wittgenstein on Some Questions in the Foundations of Mathematics," *Journal of Philosophy*, 52 (1955).

S. F. Barker, "Are Some Analytic Propositions Contingent?" *Journal of Philosophy*, 63 (1966).

R. Barrett, "Quine, Synonymy and Logical Truth," *Philosophy of Science*, 32 (1965).

C. A. Baylis, "Critique of Waismann's 'Analytic-Synthetic,'" *Journal of Symbolic Logic*, 21 (1956).

————, "Critique of S. Saito's 'Circular Definitions and Analyticity,'" *Journal of Symbolic Logic*, 27 (1962).

J. Bennett, "Analytic-Synthetic," *Proceedings of the Aristotelian Society*, N.S. 59 (1959).

G. Bergmann, "Two Types of Linguistic Philosophy," *Review of Metaphysics*, 5 (1952).

G. H. Bird, "Analytic and Synthetic," *Philosophical Quarterly*, 11 (1961).

H. Bohnert, "Carnap's Theory of Definition and Analyticity," P. A. Schilpp, *The Philosophy of Rudolf Carnap*, LaSalle, Illinois: Open Court Publishing Co., 1963.

A. Bonifacio, "Critique of Ebersole's 'On Certain Confusions in the Analytic-Synthetic Distinction,'" *Journal of Philosophy*, 53 (1956).

M. C. Bradley, "How Never to Know What You Mean," *Journal of Philosophy*, 66 (1969).

K. Britton, "Are Necessary Truths True by Convention?" *Proceedings of the Aristotelian Society* (Supplementary), 21 (1947).

C. D. Broad, "Are There Synthetic A Priori Truths?" *Proceedings of the Aristotelian Society* (Supplementary), 15 (1936).

R. C. Buck, "Clark on Natural Necessity," *Journal of Philosophy*, 62 (1965).

R. Carnap, "Reply to Criticisms," P. A. Schilpp, *The Philosophy of Rudolf Carnap*, LaSalle, Illinois: Open Court Publishing Co., 1963.

————, "Empiricism, Semantics and Ontology," *Revue Internationale de Philosophie*, 11 (1950).

————, "Meaning and Synonymy in Natural Languages," *Philosophical Studies*, 6 (1955).

L. Carroll, "What the Tortoise Said to Achilles," *Mind*, 4 (1895).

R. Cartwright, "Substitutivity," *Journal of Philosophy*, 63 (1966).

A. Church, "Carnap's Introduction to Semantics," *Philosophical Review*, 52 (1943).

R. Clark, "On What Is Naturally Necessary," *Journal of Philosophy*, 62 (1965).

B. Clarke, "Linguistic Analysis and the Philosophy of Religion," *The Monist*, 47 (1963).

L. J. Cohen, "Geach's Problem about Intentional Identity," *Journal of Philosophy*, 65 (1968).

D. C. Dennett, "Geach on Intentional Identity," *Journal of Philosophy*, 65 (1968).

F. B. Ebersole, "On Certain Confusions in the Analytic-Synthetic Distinction," *Journal of Philosophy*, 53 (1956).

R. B. Edwards, "Discussion: The Truth and Falsity of Definitions," *Philosophy of Science*, 33 (1966).

A. Ewing, "The Linguistic Theory of A Priori," *Proceedings of the Aristotelian Society*, 40 (1939–40).

H. Feigl, "The Philosophy of Science of Logical Empiricism," Neuchâtel: Ed. du Griffon, 1955, *Proceedings of the Second International Congress of the International Union for the Philosophy of Science*, I.

F. Ferre, "Color Incompatibility and Language Games," *Mind*, 70 (1961).

M. Fisk, "Analyticity and Conceptual Revision," *Journal of Philosophy*, 63 (1966).

R. E. Gahringer, "Some Observations on the Distinction between Analytic and Synthetic Propositions," *Journal of Philosophy*, 51 (1954).

N. Garver, "Criterion of Personal Identity," *Journal of Philosophy*, 61 (1964).

A. Gewirth, "The Distinction between Analytic and Synthetic Truths," *Journal of Philosophy*, 47 (1950).

N. Goodman, "On Likeness of Meaning," *Analysis*, 10 (1949).

H. P. Grice, "Utterer's Meaning and Intentions," *Philosophical Review*, 78 (1969).

———— and P. F. Strawson, "In Defense of a Dogma," *Philosophical Review*, 65 (1956).

S. C. Hackett, "Contemporary Philosophy and the Analytic-Synthetic Dichotomy," *International Philosophical Quarterly*, 7 (1967).

N. R. Hanson, "Mr. Pap on Synonymity," *Mind*, 60 (1951).

G. H. Harman, "Quine on Meaning and Existence," *Review of Metaphysics*, 21 (1967).

————, "Three Levels of Meaning," *Journal of Philosophy*, 65 (1968).

C. Hartshorne, "Necessity," *Review of Metaphysics*, 21 (1967).

W. Hay and J. Weinberg, "Concerning Allegedly Necessary Nonanalytic Propositions," *Philosophical Studies*, 2 (1951).

C. G. Hempel, "Geometry and Empirical Science," *American Mathematical Monthly*, 52 (1945).

————, "On the Nature of Mathematical Truth," *American Mathematical Monthly*, 52 (1945).

M. Hesse, "Fine's Criteria of Meaning Change," *Journal of Philosophy,* 65 (1968).

K. J. J. Hintikka, "Are Logical Truths Analytic?," *Philosophical Review,* 74 (1965).

A. Hofstadter, "Myth of the Whole," *Journal of Philosophy,* 51 (1954).

A. Kaplan, "Definition and Specification of Meaning," *Journal of Philosophy,* 43 (1946).

J. J. Katz, "Some Remarks on Quine on Analyticity," *Journal of Philosophy,* 64 (1967).

———— and E. Martin, "Synonymy of Actives and Passives," *Philosophical Review,* 76 (1967).

A. S. Kaufman, "The Analytic and the Synthetic: A Tenable Dualism," *Philosophical Review,* 62 (1953).

J. G. Kemeny, "Review of Quine's 'Two Dogmas,'" *Journal of Symbolic Logic,* 17 (1952).

————, "A New Approach to Semantics, Part I," *Journal of Symbolic Logic,* 21 (1956).

————, "Analyticity versus Fuzziness," *Synthese* (1963).

H. Langford, "A Proof that Synthetic A Priori Propositions Exist," *Journal of Philosophy,* 46 (1949).

S. Larsen, "Analyticity and Impropriety," *Journal of Philosophy,* 63 (1966).

H. Leblanc, "On Definitions," *Philosophy of Science,* 17 (1950).

C. I. Lewis, "The Modes of Meaning," *Philosophy and Phenomenological Research,* 4 (1944).

————, "The Pragmatic Conception of the A Priori," *Journal of Philosophy,* 20 (1953).

L. Linsky, "Some Notes on Carnap's Concept of Intensional Isomorphism and the Paradox of Analysis," *Philosophy of Science,* 16 (1949).

————, "Substitutivity and Descriptions," *Journal of Philosophy,* 63 (1966).

S. C. Liu, "On the Analytic and Synthetic," *Philosophical Review,* 45 (1956).

N. Malcolm, "Certainty and Empirical Statements," *Mind,* 51 (1942).

R. M. Martin, "On 'Analytic,'" *Philosophical Studies,* 3 (1952).

B. Mates, "Synonymity," *University of California Publications in Philosophy,* 25 (1950).

————, "Analytic Sentences," *Philosophical Review,* 60 (1951).

G. Maxwell, "The Necessary and the Contingent," H. Feigl and M. Scriven, *Minnesota Studies*, Vol. 3.

————, "Meaning Postulates in Scientific Theories," H. Feigl and G. Maxwell, *Current Issues in the Philosophy of Science*.

J. M. E. Moravisik, "Analytic and the Nonempirical," *Journal of Philosophy*, 62 (1965).

E. Nagel, "Logic without Ontology," Yervant H. Krikorian, *Naturalism and the Human Spirit*, Columbia University Press, 1944.

A. Pap, "The Different Kinds of A Priori," *Philosophical Review*, 53 (1944).

————, "Indubitable Existential Statements," *Mind*, 55 (1946).

————, "The Philosophical Analysis of Natural Language," *Methodos*, 1 (1949).

————, "Synonymity and Logical Equivalence," *Analysis*, 10 (1949).

————, "Are All Necessary Propositions Analytic?," *Philosophical Review*, 58 (1949).

————, "Logic and the Synthetic A Priori," *Philosophy and Phenomenological Research*, 10 (1950).

————, "Ostensive Definition and Empirical Certainty," *Mind*, 59 (1950).

————, "Belief, Synonymity, and Analysis," *Journal of Symbolic Logic*, 20 (1955).

————, "Synonymy, Identity of Concepts, and the Paradox of Analysis," *Methodos*, 7 (1955).

————, "Once More: Colors and the Synthetic A Priori," *Philosophical Review*, 56 (1957).

————, "Theory of Definition," *Philosophy of Science*, 31 (1964).

A. Pasch, "Empiricism: One 'Dogma' or Two?" *Journal of Philosophy*, 53 (1956).

D. Pears, "Incompatibilities of Colours," A. G. N. Flew, *Logic and Language, Second Series*, Oxford: Blackwell's, 1961.

J. L. Polluck, "Implications and Analyticity," *Journal of Philosophy*, 62 (1965).

H. Putnam, "Synonymity and the Analysis of Belief Sentences," *Analysis*, 14 (1954).

————, "Reds, Greens and Logical Analysis," *Philosophical Review*, 65 (1956).

————, "Reds and Greens All Over Again: A Reply to Arthur Pap," *Philosophical Review*, 66 (1957).

————, "The Analytic and Synthetic," H. Feigl and M. Scriven, *Minnesota Studies,* vol. 3.

W. Quine, "Truth by Convention," Otis H. Lee, *Philosophical Essays for A. N. Whitehead,* New York: Longmans, Green and Co., 1936.

————, "Notes on Existence and Necessity," *Journal of Philosophy,* 40 (1943).

————, "Carnap and Logical Truth," P. A. Schilpp, *The Philosophy of Rudolf Carnap,* LaSalle, Illinois: Open Court Publishing Co., 1963.

————, "Implicit Definition Sustained," *Journal of Philosophy,* 41 (1964).

C. Radford, "Ostensive Definition, Coordinative Definitions, and Necessary Empirical Statements: A Reply to Arthur Pap," *Mind,* 73 (1964).

J. Reid, "Analytic Statements in Semiosis," *Mind,* 52 (1943).

C. Rollins, "Are There Indubitable Existential Statements?," *Mind,* 58 (1949).

S. Saito, "Circular Definitions and Analyticity," *Journal of Symbolic Logic,* 22 (1962).

I. Scheffler, "On Synonymy and Indirect Discourse," *Philosophy of Science,* 22 (1955).

M. Schlick, "Meaning and Verification," *Philosophical Review,* 45 (1936).

————, "Is There a Factual A Priori?" *Wissenschaftlicher Jahresbericht der philosophischen Gesellschaft an der Universitaet zu Wien fuer das Vereinsjahr,* 1930–31.

W. Sellars, "Is There a Synthetic A Priori?," S. Hook, *American Philosophers at Work.*

————, "Putnam on Synonymity and Belief," *Analysis,* 15 (1955).

R. M. Smullyan, "Analytic Cut," *Journal of Symbolic Logic,* 33 (1968).

F. Sommers, "Meaning Relations and the Analytic," *Journal of Philosophy,* 60 (1963).

D. W. Stampe, "Toward a Grammar of Meaning," *Philosophical Review,* 77 (1968).

R. Taylor, "Disputes about Synonymy," *Philosophical Review,* 63 (1954).

S. Toulmin, "A Defense of 'Synthetic Necessary Truth,'" *Mind,* 58 (1949).

F. Waismann, "Analytic-Synthetic," *Analysis*, 10–13 (1949–52).

W. Walsh, "Analytic-Synthetic," *Proceedings of the Aristotelian Society* 54 (1953–54).

P. Weiss, "The Paradox of Necessary Truth," *Philosophical Studies*, 6 (1955).

M. Weitz, "Analytic Statements," *Mind*, 63 (1954).

M. White, "On the Church-Frege Solution of the Paradox of Analysis," *Philosophy and Phenomenological Research*, 9 (1948).

————, "On What Could Have Happened," *Philosophical Review*, 77 (1968).

————, "The Analytic and Synthetic: An Untenable Dualism," *John Dewey: Philosopher of Science and Freedom*, New York: The Dial Press, 1950.

N. L. Wilson, "Modality and Identity: A Defense," *Journal of Philosophy*, 62 (1965).

J. A. Winnie, "Theoretical Terms and Falsity of Definitions," *Philosophy of Science*, 32 (1965).

P. Ziff, "Nonsynonymy of Active and Passive Sentences," *Philosophical Review*, 75 (1966).

# QUADRANGLE PAPERBACKS

## American History

Frederick Lewis Allen. *The Lords of Creation.* (QP35)
Lewis Atherton. *Main Street on the Middle Border.* (QP36)
Thomas A. Bailey. *Woodrow Wilson and the Lost Peace.* (QP1)
Thomas A. Bailey. *Woodrow Wilson and the Great Betrayal.* (QP2)
Charles A. Beard. *The Idea of National Interest.* (QP27)
Carl L. Becker. *Everyman His Own Historian.* (QP33)
Barton J. Bernstein. *Politics and Policies of the Truman Administration.* (QP72)
Ray A. Billington. *The Protestant Crusade.* (QP12)
Allan G. Bogue. *From Prairie to Corn Belt.* (QP50)
Kenneth E. Boulding. *The Organizational Revolution.* (QP43)
Robert V. Bruce. *1877: Year of Violence.* (QP73)
Gerald M. Capers. *John C. Calhoun, Opportunist.* (QP70)
David M. Chalmers. *Hooded Americanism.* (QP51)
John Chamberlain. *Farewell to Reform.* (QP19)
Alice Hamilton Cromie. *A Tour Guide to the Civil War.*
Robert D. Cross. *The Emergence of Liberal Catholicism in America.* (QP44)
Richard M. Dalfiume. *American Politics Since 1945.* (NYTimes Book, QP57)
Carl N. Degler. *The New Deal.* (NYTimes Book, QP74)
Chester McArthur Destler. *American Radicalism, 1865-1901.* (QP30)
Robert A. Divine. *American Foreign Policy Since 1945.* (NYTimes Book, QP58)
Robert A. Divine. *Causes and Consequences of World War II.* (QP63)
Robert A. Divine. *The Illusion of Neutrality.* (QP45)
Elisha P. Douglass. *Rebels and Democrats.* (QP26)
Felix Frankfurter. *The Commerce Clause.* (QP16)
Lloyd C. Gardner. *A Different Frontier.* (QP32)
Edwin Scott Gaustad. *The Great Awakening in New England.* (QP46)
Ray Ginger. *Altgeld's America.* (QP21)
Ray Ginger. *Modern American Cities.* (NYTimes Book, QP67)
Ray Ginger. *Six Days or Forever?* (QP68)
Gerald N. Grob. *Workers and Utopia.* (QP61)
Louis Hartz. *Economic Policy and Democratic Thought.* (QP52)
William B. Hesseltine. *Lincoln's Plan of Reconstruction.* (QP41)
Granville Hicks. *The Great Tradition.* (QP62)
Dwight W. Hoover. *Understanding Negro History.* (QP49)
Stanley P. Hirshson. *Farewell to the Bloody Shirt.* (QP53)
Frederic C. Howe. *The Confessions of a Reformer.* (QP39)
Harold L. Ickes. *The Autobiography of a Curmudgeon.* (QP69)
Louis Joughin and Edmund M. Morgan. *The Legacy of Sacco and Vanzetti.* (QP7)
William Loren Katz. *Teachers' Guide to American Negro History.* (QP210)
Burton Ira Kaufman. *Washington's Farewell Address.* (QP64)
Edward Chase Kirkland. *Dream and Thought in the Business Community, 1860-1900.* (QP11)
Edward Chase Kirkland. *Industry Comes of Age.* (QP42)
Adrienne Koch. *The Philosophy of Thomas Jefferson.* (QP17)
Gabriel Kolko. *The Triumph of Conservatism.* (QP40)
Walter LaFeber. *John Quincy Adams and American Continental Empire.* (QP23)
Lawrence H. Leder. *The Meaning of the American Revolution.* (NYTimes Book, QP66)
David E. Lilienthal. *TVA: Democracy on the March.* (QP28)
Arthur S. Link. *Wilson the Diplomatist.* (QP18)
Huey P. Long. *Every Man a King.* (QP8)
Gene M. Lyons. *America: Purpose and Power.* (QP24)
Jackson Turner Main. *The Antifederalists.* (QP14)
Ernest R. May. *The World War and American Isolation, 1914-1917.* (QP29)
Henry F. May. *The End of American Innocence.* (QP9)
Thomas J. McCormick. *China Market.* (QP75)
George E. Mowry. *The California Progressives.* (QP6)
William L. O'Neill. *American Society Since 1945.* (NYTimes Book, QP59)
Frank L. Owsley. *Plain Folk of the Old South.* (QP22)
David Graham Phillips. *The Treason of the Senate.* (QP20)
Julius W. Pratt. *Expansionists of 1898.* (QP15)
C. Herman Pritchett. *The Roosevelt Court.* (QP71)
Moses Rischin. *The American Gospel of Success.* (QP54)
John P. Roche. *The Quest for the Dream.* (QP47)
David A. Shannon. *The Socialist Party of America.* (QP38)
Andrew Sinclair. *The Available Man.* (QP60)

## American History (continued)

John Spargo. *The Bitter Cry of the Children.* (QP55)
Bernard Sternsher. *The Negro in Depression and War.* (QP65)
Richard W. Van Alstyne. *The Rising American Empire.* (QP25)
Willard M. Wallace. *Appeal to Arms.* (QP10)
Norman Ware. *The Industrial Worker, 1840-1860.* (QP13)
Albert K. Weinberg. *Manifest Destiny.* (QP3)
Bernard A. Weisberger. *They Gathered at the River.* (QP37)
Robert H. Wiebe. *Businessmen and Reform.* (QP56)
William Appleman Williams. *The Contours of American History.* (QP34)
William Appleman Williams. *The Great Evasion.* (QP48)
Esmond Wright. *Causes and Consequences of the American Revolution.* (QP31)

## European History

William Sheridan Allen. *The Nazi Seizure of Power.* (QP302)
W. O. Henderson. *The Industrial Revolution in Europe.* (QP303)
Raul Hilberg. *The Destruction of the European Jews.* (QP301)
Richard N. Hunt. *German Social Democracy.* (QP306)
Telford Taylor. *Sword and Swastika.* (QP304)
John Weiss. *Nazis and Fascists in Europe, 1918-1945.* (NYTimes Book, QP305)

## Philosophy

F. H. Bradley. *The Presuppositions of Critical History.* (QP108)
William Earle. *Objectivity.* (QP109)
James M. Edie, James P. Scanlan, Mary-Barbara Zeldin, George L. Kline. *Russian Philosophy.* (3 vols, QP111, 112, 113)
James M. Edie. *An Invitation to Phenomenology.* (QP103)
James M. Edie. *New Essays in Phenomenology.* (QP114)
James M. Edie. *Phenomenology in America.* (QP105)
R. O. Elveton. *The Phenomenology of Husserl.* (QP116)
Manfred S. Frings. *Heidegger and the Quest for Truth.* (QP107)
Moltke S. Gram. *Kant: Disputed Questions.* (QP104)
James F. Harris, Jr., and Richard Severens. *Analyticity.* (QP117)
E. D. Klemke. *Studies in the Philosophy of G. E. Moore.* (QP115)
Lionel Rubinoff. *Faith and Reason.* (QP106)
Stuart F. Spicker. *The Philosophy of the Body.* (QP118)
Paul Tibbetts. *Perception.* (QP110)
Pierre Thévenaz. *What Is Phenomenology?* (QP101)

## Social Science

Shalom Endleman. *Violence in the Streets.* (QP215)
Nathan Glazer. *Cities in Trouble.* (NYTimes Book, QP212)
George and Eunice Grier. *Equality and Beyond.* (QP204)
Kurt Lang and Gladys Engel Lang. *Politics and Television.* (QP216)
Charles O. Lerche, Jr. *Last Chance in Europe.* (QP207)
Raymond W. Mack. *Prejudice and Race Relations.* (NYTimes Book, QP217)
David Mitrany. *A Working Peace System.* (QP205)
H. L. Nieburg. *In the Name of Science.* (QP218)
Martin Oppenheimer. *The Urban Guerrilla.* (QP219)
Martin Oppenheimer and George Lakey. *A Manual for Direct Action.* (QP202)
James Parkes. *Antisemitism.* (QP213)
Fred Powledge. *To Change a Child.* (QP209)
Lee Rainwater. *And the Poor Get Children.* (QP208)
*The Rockefeller Report on the Americas.* (QP214)
Clarence Senior. *The Puerto Ricans.* (QP201)
Harold L. Sheppard. *Poverty and Wealth in America.* (NYTimes Book, QP220)
Arthur L. Stinchcombe. *Rebellion in a High School.* (QP211)
Harry M. Trebing. *The Corporation in the American Economy.* (NYTimes Book, QP221)
David Manning White. *Pop Culture in America.* (NYTimes Book, QP222)